"*Political Thought* is a wonderful introduction to the study of politics. Hunter Baker writes as a true teacher, offering not only rigor and clarity but also a personal touch. He shows his reader that the study of political thought is not just an abstract exercise for dreary academics, but an application of practical reason to the question of how we are to live together in freedom and order to advance the common good. While introducing the student to the greatest political philosophers in history, Professor Baker takes great care in showing the indelible marks these thinkers have left on our civilization, and how they, for good or ill, have shaped the way Christians should critically assess their place in civil society and its political institutions."

Francis J. Beckwith, Professor of Philosophy and Church-State Studies, Baylor University; author, *Politics for Christians*

"What is the purpose of politics? How should we order our lives together? In lively and engaging prose, Hunter Baker surveys the answers that great thinkers have given to these enduring questions. His book is an excellent, accessible introduction to the fundamental themes of political discourse—and to why these matter for the rising generation."

George H. Nash, author, *The Conservative Intellectual Movement in America Since 1945*

"Hunter Baker provides an accessible and insightful primer on the various streams of thought and action at play in American public life. A notable merit of Baker's work is that it examines clear alternatives while at the same time doing justice to the dynamic variety in and between different schools of thought. Baker paints a clear and compelling picture of the political landscape and in so doing provides a valuable service both for those learning about politics for the first time and for those seeking a refresher and a summary of political thought."

Jordan J. Ballor, Research Fellow, Acton Institute for the Study of Religion & Liberty; author, *Ecumenical Babel*

~SERIES ENDORSEMENTS~

POLITICAL THOUGHT

RECLAIMING THE
CHRISTIAN INTELLECTUAL TRADITION

David S. Dockery, series editor

CONSULTING EDITORS

Hunter Baker
Timothy George
Niel Nielson
Philip G. Ryken
Michael J. Wilkins
John D. Woodbridge

OTHER RCIT VOLUMES

The Great Tradition of Christian Thinking, David S. Dockery and
    Timothy George
The Liberal Arts, Gene C. Fant Jr.
Literature, Louis Markos
Philosophy, David K. Naugle

POLITICAL THOUGHT
A STUDENT'S GUIDE

Hunter Baker

CROSSWAY

WHEATON, ILLINOIS

Political Thought: A Student's Guide

Copyright © 2012 by Hunter Baker

Published by Crossway
         1300 Crescent Street
         Wheaton, Illinois 60187

Cover design: Jon McGrath, Simplicated Studio

First printing 2012

Printed in the United States of America

Scripture quotations are from the ESV® Bible (*The Holy Bible, English Standard Version*®), copyright © 2001 by Crossway. Used by permission. All rights reserved.

Trade paperback ISBN: 978-1-4335-3119-4
PDF ISBN: 978-1-4335-3120-0
Mobipocket ISBN: 978-1-4335-3121-7
ePub ISBN: 978-1-4335-3122-4

Library of Congress Cataloging-in-Publication Data

Baker, Hunter, 1970-.
Political thought : a student's guide / Hunter Baker.
  p. cm.—(Reclaiming the Christian intellectual tradition)
  Includes index.
  ISBN 978-1-4335-3119-4 (tp)
  1. Christianity and politics. 2. Christian sociology. 3. Political science—Philosophy. I. Title.
BR115.P7B144   2012
261.7—dc23   2012001369

Crossway is a publishing ministry of Good News Publishers.

VP		20	19	18	17	16	15	14	13	12
14	13	12	11	10	9	8	7	6	5	4	3	2	1

To Ruth Baker,
the good wife, and mother of my children
whom I love and find irreplaceable,

and

Jack Roady,
the new district attorney of Galveston County
and the best friend I have ever had.

CONTENTS

SERIES PREFACE

RECLAIMING THE CHRISTIAN INTELLECTUAL TRADITION

The Reclaiming the Christian Intellectual Tradition series is designed to provide an overview of the distinctive way the church has read the Bible, formulated doctrine, provided education, and engaged the culture. The contributors to this series all agree that personal faith and genuine Christian piety are essential for the life of Christ followers and for the church. These contributors also believe that helping others recognize the importance of serious thinking about God, Scripture, and the world needs a renewed emphasis at this time in order that the truth claims of the Christian faith can be passed along from one generation to the next. The study guides in this series will enable us to see afresh how the Christian faith shapes how we live, how we think, how we write books, how we govern society, and how we relate to one another in our churches and social structures. The richness of the Christian intellectual tradition provides guidance for the complex challenges that believers face in this world.

This series is particularly designed for Christian students and others associated with college and university campuses, including faculty, staff, trustees, and other various constituents. The contributors to the series will explore how the Bible has been interpreted in the history of the church, as well as how theology has been formulated. They will ask: How does the Christian faith influence our understanding of culture, literature, philosophy, government, beauty, art, or work? How does the Christian intellectual tradition help us understand truth? How does the Christian intellectual tradition shape our approach to education? We believe that this series is not only timely but that it meets an important need, because the secular culture in which we now find ourselves is, at best, indifferent to the Christian faith, and the Christian world— at least in its more popular forms—tends to be confused about the beliefs, heritage, and tradition associated with the Christian faith. At the heart of this work is the challenge to prepare a generation of Christians to think Christianly, to engage the academy and the culture, and to serve church and society. We believe that both the breadth and the depth of the Christian intellectual tradition need to be reclaimed, revitalized, renewed, and revived for us to carry forward this work. These study guides will seek to provide a framework to help introduce students to the great tradition of Christian thinking, seeking to highlight its importance for understanding the world, its significance for serving both church and society, and its application for Christian thinking and learning. The series is a starting point for exploring important ideas and issues such as truth, meaning, beauty, and justice.

We trust that the series will help introduce readers to the apostles, church fathers, Reformers, philosophers, theologians, historians, and a wide variety of other significant thinkers. In addition to well-known leaders such as Clement, Origen, Augustine, Thomas Aquinas, Martin Luther, and Jonathan Edwards, readers will be pointed to William Wilberforce, G. K. Chesterton, T. S. Eliot, Dorothy Sayers, C. S. Lewis, Johann Sebastian Bach, Isaac Newton, Johannes Kepler, George Washington Carver, Elizabeth Fox-Genovese, Michael Polanyi, Henry Luke Orombi, and many others. In doing so, we hope to introduce those who throughout history have demonstrated that it is indeed possible to be serious about the life of the mind while simultaneously being deeply committed Christians. These efforts to strengthen serious Christian thinking and scholarship will not be limited to the study of theology, scriptural interpretation, or philosophy, even though these areas provide the framework for understanding the Christian faith for all other areas of exploration. In order for us to reclaim and advance the Christian intellectual tradition, we must have some understanding of the tradition itself. The volumes in this series will seek to explore this tradition and its application for our twenty-first-century world. Each volume contains helpful tools, such as a glossary, study questions, and a list of resources for further study, which we trust will provide helpful guidance for our readers.

I am deeply grateful to the series editorial committee: Timothy George, John Woodbridge, Michael Wilkins, Niel Nielson, Philip Ryken, and Hunter Baker. Each of these colleagues joins me in thanking our various contributors for their fine work. We all express our appreciation to Justin Taylor, Jill Carter, Allan Fisher, Lane Dennis, and the Crossway team for their enthusiastic support for the project. We offer the project with the hope that students will be helped, faculty and Christian leaders will be encouraged, institutions will be strengthened, churches will be built up, and, ultimately, that God will be glorified.

Soli Deo Gloria
David S. Dockery,
Series Editor

AUTHOR'S PREFACE

There are many ways one could go about writing an introductory text on political thought. Because this book is part of a series of volumes intentionally written to offer brief invitations to different academic subjects, I have chosen not to structure the book as a survey of the major thinkers.

Instead, I have elected to introduce readers to political thought through the use of familiar life circumstances, imaginative devices, and a discussion of the great themes, which have been important and remain so. Therefore, this is a book that ranges across things such as the family, the state of nature, order, justice, freedom, and Christianity.

It is my hope that the discussion will prove stimulating and that many who read this book will decide to make further and more detailed study in the area of political philosophy. Regardless, serious consideration of the issues raised here will lead to greater capacity for evaluating political proposals and the claims that go with them. I knew I was on the right track with this book when my wife, who has long had very little interest in politics and is very scientifically minded, read the manuscript and subsequently told me she suddenly began to see the things I had described in the text everywhere in the news.

The reader may even feel empowered to independently agree with or take issue with the author! And nothing would make him happier.

ACKNOWLEDGMENTS

In the preface to my first book, *The End of Secularism*, I offered a tribute to Richard John Neuhaus in the wake of his then-recent passing. More than anyone, he (through his writings) taught me a way of looking at matters of church and state that led me into a career of writing and teaching.

On the occasion of the publication of this book, I would like to honor the life and memory of William F. Buckley Jr., who founded *National Review*, hosted the fantastic public affairs program *Firing Line* on PBS for many years, and compiled a mountain of articles, books, and speeches in the course of his public career. Buckley died a few years ago, but that is nothing that should stop a fellow Christian (and supernaturalist) from expressing gratitude!

Like Neuhaus, Buckley was not an academic but was instead the kind of hugely influential figure who models wit and erudition for the educated public and thus inspires more people than will ever be known on this side of heaven to follow in his footsteps and to read, learn, and write. I will never forget his visit to the University of Georgia when I was a graduate student in the early 1990s (especially his unforgettable answer to a questioner who asked him what he thought of Rush Limbaugh—he was humorously affirming in his response). Never has there been a time when I sat so far on the edge of my seat or listened harder to a speaker. I had to do so in order to capture every jewel issuing forth from the man wearing what appeared to be a fire engine–red belt (perhaps honoring the Georgia Bulldogs!). Or so it is in the film reel of memory.

I would also like to offer my gratitude to another man who has left us behind in this life, Russell Kirk. Through his books, I learned to understand ordered liberty. He only taught briefly at what was then called Michigan State College (now Michigan State University) before he went on to become an independent man of letters for the Western world. Due to his prodigious output (and the commercial success of his ghost stories such as *The Old House of Fear*), he was able to make a living at it. I hope this book will inspire an interest in political thought sufficient to encourage readers to move on to his wonderful (and large) *The Roots of American Order*. In that magnum opus, he traced our political culture through four cities: Jerusalem, Athens, Rome, and London. Read it and find out why.

So much for the men I never knew but profited greatly from reading. I also owe a continuing debt to men I *have* known such as David Dockery, Robert Sloan, Francis Beckwith, Barry Hankins, Donald Schmeltekopf, David Lyle Jeffrey, and James Bennighof. Without their encouragement and help, I have no idea where I would be today. Probably not writing this book. I would also like to acknowledge the friendship of my colleagues in political science at Union University: Micah Watson (who offered comments on one of the chapters), Sean Evans, and Greg Ryan, and my old colleagues at Houston Baptist University: Chris Hammons and Michael Bordelon (both missed for their good humor and insightfulness).

As is the tradition with acknowledgment sections in books, I am quick to add that while individuals mentioned here deserve credit for anything good or edifying the reader might encounter, any mistakes or other infelicities are my sole responsibility.

SECTION 1

WAYS TO BEGIN THINKING ABOUT POLITICS

1

BEGINNING WITH THE FAMILIAR

Aristotle famously identified the family as the primary unit of political society. One might be tempted to object and insist on the primacy of the individual, but the Greek philosopher's reasoning was that there is no society without the family. Hillary Clinton wrote a book on the theme of an African proverb that says, "It takes a village to raise a child." Aristotle insisted, more basically, that it takes a family to form the basis of the broader society.[1]

Whether one centers political analysis on the individual, the family, the village, the nation-state, or the world community, the family is the first place in which we must interact with each other. It is our first society. The novelist Pat Conroy once said that each divorce results in the death of a small civilization.[2] And he is right.

In part because of these reasons, I would like to begin our thinking about political thought with some personal reflections on family. My other motivation is that this is an introductory text. Many people are intimidated by phrases such as *political thought* or *political philosophy*. If we begin by talking about something virtually all of us can understand, such as the family, we can take a subject that may seem overly complicated or cerebral and make it more accessible. Families have features such as leadership, order, fairness, debate, restrictions, coercion, and freedoms. There are priorities, decisions, boundaries, budgets, and many other aspects

---

[1] Aristotle, *Politics*, bk. 1, chap. 2. (I will follow this form of quoting certain classical texts that have long been in the public domain and are available in many different editions.)
[2] Pat Conroy, "Requiem for a Marriage," *Reader's Digest*, January 1988, 109–12.

that mirror political life. Rather than speak of families generally, I propose to talk about mine and the one in which my wife was raised. Through our experiences, you will be able to spot some fundamental ideas about politics.

I was raised in a family that had and has its own way of doing things. In this family, I had a great deal of freedom to decide what I was going to do. I don't mean that I determined my own bedtime or made my own rules, but rather that I had the discretion to figure out what to do with my time outside of musts such as attending school.

While our family often ate together, sometimes we didn't. On occasion, my folks would eat and talk in the kitchen while my sister and I ate sandwiches of our own heterodox design in front of the television (white bread, sliced ham, and A-1 steak sauce!). There were large unstructured patches of time available in any given day. I spent many happy hours alone in my room reading comic books, building with Legos, creating tents out of sheets and folding chairs, and even writing stories at my little desk. Other times, I wandered outside just looking around or playing games of imagination. Through sheer repetition over long hours, I taught myself how to play basketball by heaving up endless shots toward the hoop that seemed so far away when I began. I learned tennis in a similar fashion, beating fuzzy green spheres into the masonry on the side of our house and learning how to predict their rebound.

There were also more structured periods. I often had baseball practices and games to attend. My father and I regularly played catch for about thirty minutes or an hour after he came home from work. Friends and I frequently organized pickup games of football (we played it full contact with no pads or helmets) in each other's yard.

The overriding theme of my childhood was bounded freedom. There were limits all around me. I had to finish homework. I had to be in bed by a certain time (reading if not sleeping). I had to go to school. A number of family activities were not optional. But what I remember so clearly was the great liberty I had to pursue my interests and desires. My family was a happy one, though it bucked the typical image by being one in which each member had a lot of time to him- or herself. I loved that.

The life I had as a child is a good example of a political idea that has had special resonance in America. The idea is ordered liberty. Ordered liberty means that to the degree a person is willing to govern himself, he can be free of a lot of external control over the details of his life. In other words, part of the reason I may have had a lot of liberty in my childhood is that I had little tendency to misuse it. (Committing acts of mischief never held any attraction for me. My internal moral compass was fairly strong.) In this way of thinking, we move toward the true meaning of liberty. We tend to think of liberty as a synonym for freedom or an absolute release from constraints of any kind, but to do so is to fail to think deeply enough. It is true that words such as *liberty* and *confinement* are effectively opposites, but it is also true that "liberty" is often opposed to another word, which is *license*. Used in this way, license refers to a wrong use of freedom or a wrong direction of human agency. Liberty implies a correct use of freedom.

Before I go further, I must admit that there are some drawbacks to the type of upbringing I describe. My folks did not exercise a great deal of control over the books I read, shows I watched, music I listened to, or videos my friends and I rented. (The one real constraint I recall is my father personally asking me not to see the film *The Exorcist* because of the disturbing images he recalled from the movie. Without question, I honored the request and still do.) In the course of the high school years, I probably consumed a lot of books and other media that were less than appropriate for a young person. And that kind of thing, of course, is one of the costs of freedom.

My wife, on the other hand, grew up in a different sort of

family. Her comings and goings were more limited. Her parents made firm rules about things such as the kind of music she could listen to. Popular music in the style of Top 40 rock and roll was off-limits. They had a much stronger bent toward group activity. Freedom was less of a value than living out a certain type of excellence that was centered on being a good Christian. For her family, this meant avoiding a variety of influences that were viewed as corrupting or worldly. It also meant choosing to spend a great deal of time doing things such as memorizing Scripture. The family also put a lot of work into traveling together and developing a record of memorable experiences as a group. Unsurprisingly, they achieved what they set out to do. They are a tightly bound unit with an incredible collection of slide shows from their journeys!

Based on the description I've offered so far, you can see that my wife's family was not about something like ordered liberty in the way mine was. In the Baker family individuals had wide discretion in how to order their lives as long as they avoided crashing certain boundary lines. Instead, her family identified a specific type of excellence centered on group participation and Christianity. The parents provided substantial guidance (and good, old-fashioned parental coercion) in that direction with the goal of producing the desired result. If we were to associate a political ideal with her family, it would be something like civic excellence or civic idealism.

Today when we visit her family, I experience a bit of culture shock (something that is not unusual for those who cross family lines via marriage). Now, the dissonance I feel is not centered on the Christian confession that I have come to embrace. The trouble for me is that for a period of several days I have to reconcile my own desire for broad discretion and liberty with my wife's family ideal of group participation. I want to wander, go off by myself for a couple of hours, and just make sure I get back for the important parts. To me, that sort of accountability to the group seems perfectly reasonable. To them, especially the women, my model represents preferring the self to the group and rejecting the collective effort to make memories together.

My wife experiences a parallel but opposite sort of disconnect when she is the Martin among the Bakers. We get together at some rented cabin or at my parents' home, where people pretty much break off and do what they want. There are times when we all gather for some meal or activity, but there is a great deal of spinning away from the nucleus as individuals or subgroups and charting separate paths in the context of the overall family vacation. Having grown up in a very different type of family, she feels as though the activities are too fragmented and that there is not enough togetherness. For her, love expresses itself through careful planning and cohesiveness, but my family tends to feel happy and reunited sharing the same general area and periodically doing something as a group.

You may be reading this and thinking the description is very personal and not really related to politics, but what I am describing in terms of different types of families and the ways they interact is the same fundamental dynamic that is present in politics. Both types of people (and other types!) live together in political communities. The same values and instincts contend with one another. Should we all be highly plugged into a community collectivity with our lives tightly wound together (often in nonoptional ways)? Or should we place a very high value on individual discretion? What is more important?

As the next short chapter will demonstrate, families are not synonymous with political societies and should not be confused as such. However, the dynamics of freedom, discretion, group activity, individual and joint identification of ideals, supervision, and control all apply in both the family and the political community. For that reason, thinking about how things were in your family is not a bad way of beginning to evaluate political life.

2

THE DIFFERENCE BETWEEN FAMILIES AND POLITICAL COMMUNITIES

The society grows directly out of the family. Aristotle described a process wherein the family spins off other families. This group of families becomes a village. Villages eventually merge into towns. We can see the merger between paternal power and political power in the similarity between the word for relatives (*kin*) and the word for the chief of the race or tribe (*king*).[1]

Indeed, one of the great political problems for the ages has been to determine the degree to which political power should be similar to paternal/maternal power. At the height of the power of monarchies, kings and queens certainly did consider themselves to be something like fathers and mothers of their people. And just as children do not understand everything that is necessary for them to grow and flourish, so, too (the logic went), did the subjects of monarchs lack the capacity to act on their own behalf.

Though throughout much of Western civilization people have enjoyed certain rights that bear some similarity to what we think of as modern democracy, it was not until fairly recently (historically speaking) that the hold of monarchical and aristocratic power was decisively broken in the West. In the wave of breaking away, John Locke argued that paternal power and political power are not the same thing. Grown human beings are not comparable

[1]Aristotle, *Politics*, bk. 1, chap. 2.

to children in their capacities relative to parents. Instead, they are mature, rational creatures very much like those who would claim the right to rule them. So, though the political society comes into existence through and is sustained by the family, it is not synonymous with the family. Citizens are not children and are not equally subject to coercion (even in their interest) in the same way as children are.[2]

And so, in terms of our historical drift, we have moved away from the tendency (whether enforced or organic) to view political power as paternal power. We look at ourselves as free and rational individuals capable of making decisions about the community matters that affect us and about how we should lead our own lives. But the question of how we will live together (an alternate phrasing of Francis Schaeffer's famous *How Shall We Then Live?*) remains.

Free individuals still have to make choices about community life as their paths almost inevitably cross. Indeed, we find that we can better satisfy our wants and needs within the context of mutual relationship with other human beings. Thomas Paine called the voluntary phase of this relationship "society" and referred to the necessary evil of the involuntary part of living together as "government."[3] The question boils down to something like, *How big do we want this involuntary part to be?*

---

[2]John Locke, *Second Treatise of Government*, chaps. 1 and 6.
[3]Thomas Paine, *Common Sense*. Paine's valuable and much-reprinted essay may be found at http://www.constitution.org/civ/comsense.htm.

3

STATES OF NATURE AND SOCIAL CONTRACTS

I began our consideration of the matter of political theory—which some find intimidating—through discussion of the family. We can all understand the family.

There is another device that can help us understand political thought. Many theorists have employed it. The device is political reasoning based on the state of nature. In other words, what kind of politics would human beings have if they lost all of their encrustations of family status, wealth, and tradition? What if we could wipe the slate clean? How would human beings move from nature to government?

One of the most popular television programs of the last decade, *Lost*, began with a jetliner crashing on a mysterious island in the middle of the Pacific. Some of the episodes dealt with issues of how strangers stripped of the accoutrements of civilization would live together. (Don't worry: there are no serious spoilers here for those who intend to watch the show.)

To give an example, consider a character introduced to us as "Sawyer." After the plane crashes and people are recovering from shock and taking care of each other, Sawyer rummages through the remains of the aircraft and luggage and creates a cache of medicine, tools, books, and other items that he keeps to himself. He forcefully insists these items are his property. One of the fundamental tensions in the early shows revolves around his claim. Others don't recognize his claim as a morally legitimate one.

Sawyer resorts to the threat of force to keep what he has taken. The situation portrayed is useful in helping us think about property. What is it? When do we think someone has a right to it? What makes property claims legitimate?

In another story line, one of the characters decides to try to reform Sawyer. He tells him that the other members of the mini-civilization are thinking of banishing him from their midst. Sawyer is a hard man who doesn't see things others' way. At first, he intends to simply leave because he will only live on his own terms. Then he realizes that he may actually need others to help him live. He tries to fish and comes up empty-handed. Upon recognizing that he is somewhat dependent on other members of the community, he makes efforts to show kindness and avoid banishment. The story here teaches us that we are not fully self-contained individuals. Yes, we have our own minds and abilities, but we do not truly live apart from others. We need each other in a variety of ways, many of them never realized because of how much we take for granted. It begins when we are children, who need our parents, and continues throughout our lives as the fruits of cooperation make it easier for us both to survive and to achieve our own goals. What does this interdependence mean for government? What are the just bounds of community imperatives? What are the rights of the individual?

THE SOCIAL CONTRACT THINKERS

The famed social contract thinkers—Thomas Hobbes, John Locke, and Jean-Jacques Rousseau—used the state of nature as a device for figuring out the just claims of the state against the freedom of the individual. Social contracts are cessions of some portion of personal sovereignty by individuals to a government in exchange for the superior protection of the rest of their rights and freedoms. We leave the state of nature to enter political society. While it is true that we give up our autonomy, we gain certain protections that should be worth the trade.

Their efforts were driven by a couple of important social developments. All three men came from a Europe that was marred by the religious wars that followed the Reformation. Although it is true that the Reformation successfully curbed many of the abuses that the Catholic church of the time engaged in and brought about a more democratized Christianity in which many could access the Scriptures, one of the negative results was a degree of political destabilization. The reforms completely disrupted the old formula of one king, one people, and one church. At times, the Catholic Church and monarchs had battled each other, but the Reformation complicated things further. Now, different nations had different churches. Rulers embraced versions of the Christian faith that were sometimes at odds with the preferences of many of the people. Tolerance of religious differences was not a characteristic of European culture at the time. Persecution and war were the preferred methods of restoring equilibrium to the old order.

In addition, Europeans were dealing with the claims of monarchs as they had for centuries. To what degree are people empowered to choose their ruler? Are monarchs free to hand their authority down to heirs? Do rulers have power over matters such as religion, publication, and opinion? By stripping politics down to its bare essence through the device of the state of nature, these thinkers (Hobbes, Locke, and Rousseau) sought to solve the problems of religious difference and to determine the justice of claims of rulers.

THOMAS HOBBES

Much depends on each thinker's perception of man's life in the state of nature. Consider Thomas Hobbes. If Hobbes could fill out the levels of Abraham Maslow's famous hierarchy of needs, he would identify freedom from violent death as the fundamental level at the bottom of the pyramid. Hobbes pondered the state of nature and concluded that it would be a dangerous place. All men are approximately equal. While it is true that men are not actually equal in terms of their intelligence, their physical strength, and in other important ways, Hobbes was thinking about a different kind of equality. This equality comes from the social fact that almost any man could kill any other man under the right set of circumstances. The motive for these murders could be almost anything, but the dominant cause would be conflicting wants. Whenever two human beings (or more) want the same thing, they have reason to kill their competition and take it. As a result, every human being in a state of nature reasonably fears being killed by one of his fellows. Under such conditions, the life of man would be "solitary, poor, nasty, brutish, and short."[1]

If only we had a common power to overawe us, then order could be restored. We need to abandon our equality in nature to kill each other and exchange it for a new kind of equality. In our new equality, we will be equally under the power of Leviathan. Leviathan is an awesomely powerful state. Leviathan could be a man or a governing body. The point of the name is to communicate the massive strength that must be reposed in the structure. What was impossible in the state of nature because of constant danger and uncertainty—things such as industry, agriculture, navigation, and all other manner of arts and science—can be achieved with Leviathan protecting all from all and establishing comprehensive order.[2]

Leviathan demands that all power be centered in the government. Once consent has been granted in its formation, it will never be asked again. The sovereign authority need not even obey its own laws, because its will, by definition, is law. There is no freedom of speech, no freedom of the press, no freedom of religion. These things are too powerful to be entrusted to the people. They are potential causes of disorder. Instead, Leviathan will manage

[1]Thomas Hobbes, *Leviathan*, pt. 1, chap. 13.
[2]Ibid., pt. 1, chaps. 13–17.

the dissemination of information. Leviathan will determine the correct religion for all.[3] Standing in our current position in a world where government's possible reach has been extended dramatically by technology, Hobbes's solution to the problem of conflicting desires looks a lot like George Orwell's nightmarish totalitarian state in *1984*.

Nevertheless, Hobbes does deserve some credit for coming up with an answer. If disagreement and disorder become deadly, which they have certainly done at times, then centralizing power and control in one place offers a swift way to restore order. If you value order and physical safety very highly, then Hobbes's answer makes some sense. Certainly, when human affairs devolve into chaos, the Hobbesian solution is one to which we tend to turn. See Napoleon after the French Revolution. See Adolf Hitler after the humiliation of Germany in the wake of World War I. See Chairman Mao after the Chinese Revolution. See Fidel Castro after the Cuban Revolution. See (perhaps) Vladimir Putin in Russia today. Sometimes, the chaos emerges by accident. At other times, it has been engineered by those hoping to play the role of Leviathan.

Each thinker has his own dominant theme, a political value that trumps the rest. For Hobbes, it is order.

JEAN-JACQUES ROUSSEAU

Jean-Jacques Rousseau stands a pole apart from Hobbes. He envisions the state of nature quite differently. In Rousseau's mind, men fare reasonably well in nature. Those who are weak obviously don't last long, but those who survive will find themselves thriving. These men are nearly superhuman. They can see much farther than their modern descendants. They have far more acute senses of smell and hearing. Armed with a stout tree branch, they are the equals of a wolf or a bear. At the same time, their desires are few.

---

[3]Ibid., pt. 1, chap. 21.

Natural men only want food when they are hungry, a place to rest under a tree at night, and limited encounters with the opposite sex to satisfy primal urges.

According to Rousseau, men have only two points on their natural moral compass. The first is to evade pain and death for themselves. The second is enough human pity not to want to see others harmed if it can be avoided. Thus, the limit of their social instinct will be to interact with the opposite sex when hormones trigger desire and to come to the aid of other human beings if it can be done without excessive risk to their own lives. He did not imagine families in nature. Men do not stay with women to raise children. They do not necessarily even see a causal connection between their sexual activity and reproduction. So, man wanders free with simple desires and virtually no social obligations. This is the famed Rousseauian noble savage.[4]

Under the state of affairs as Rousseau viewed them through the prism of deep antiquity, there is no reason to empower a Leviathan to bring peace and order so that man can develop industry, agriculture, commerce, arts, letters, and society. Indeed, these things will only bring man misery as he loses his simple life with few wants and needs. Worse yet, the development of culture will lead to inequality among men. The formation of society represents nothing less than the fall of man from a quasi-edenic state of grace. All of those things that Hobbes counted as goods to be protected were viewed by Rousseau as consequences of the fall from innocence.

Reading Rousseau's *Discourse on Inequality* in which he spelled out this view of things, one faces a question of whether to take him literally. Does he really think primitivism is better? Does he really take such a dismissive view of the family? Certainly, in reading the *Discourse* one can see the inspiration for certain ideas that began to hold sway among young people in the 1960s. The desire to throw off taboos about sex and nudity, to embrace

---

[4]Jean-Jacques Rousseau, *Discourse on Inequality*, pt. 1.

nature, to question social structures as sources of inequality—all of these can be traced back to Rousseau. Now, still a better question is whether he really meant it. Did Rousseau think we should all return to our savage roots and become the sort of men so simple as to sell a bedroll in the morning and weep for the lack of it at night? Or was he after something else?

Looking at his *The Social Contract*, one gets the sense that Rousseau's speculations about the state of nature and man's happy place in it were simply designed to set the stage for more advantageous negotiations. Rather than rolling back the clock and doing away with almost all of the things that compose our life together, he was really arguing for a different vision of government. In nature, we are equal. In society, we should be equal too.

The form this equality takes is participation in government. Rousseau argued that we should keep our political communities small enough (perhaps no bigger than could fit in a stadium) so that we could all take part in making laws. Out of our collective deliberations will come the general will. Indeed, the goal of meeting together is not so much to enunciate our individual opinion as it is to predict what the general will is and to cast a vote in that direction. He deals with the problem of oppressive majoritarianism by limiting the consideration of the people to very general matters. No bill of specificity such that it would benefit a particular group at the expense of another would be a suitable agenda item. To be part of the general will is to be free. If one is wrong about the general will, then Rousseau proclaimed one must be made to be free by being made to join it! So, the benefit of the social contract is not so much in the attainment of physical protection or of one's property but in the maintenance of one's status as a decision maker with input like the others in the group.[5]

It is interesting that although Rousseau began from a radically different place than Hobbes vis-à-vis the state of nature, he arrived

---

[5] Jean-Jacques Rousseau, *The Social Contract*, bk. 2, chap. 6.

at a similar place in terms of the power of government. A government empowered by the general will is strong, indeed. It is, in fact, a government that will exclude "competition" from an entity such as "Roman Christianity" (as he referred to Catholicism) for the minds and souls of men. A church claiming an independent standing creates an unhelpful conflict among citizens. They do not know whom to obey. The answer is a civil religion with deistic nods toward eternal rewards and punishments for good and evil. The only heresy is intolerance of the sort that would believe another citizen is going to hell. Rousseau believed no one could reasonably live with men they thought were destined for perdition.[6] There are certain echoes of our modern attitude here. But the broader point is that Rousseau, like Hobbes, envisioned a government so powerful that it could regulate religious belief.

Rousseau's dominant theme is related to Hobbes's but has a different emphasis. His primary political value is equality, which is a significant factor in our perception of justice.

JOHN LOCKE

Between these two titans of political philosophy stands the figure of John Locke. And he, at least from the perspective of our own day and the past couple hundred years, has proven to be the most influential of the three. It is possible that many readers will recognize the name John Locke as one belonging to a key character in the television show *Lost*, which was mentioned earlier. Regrettably, there is no obvious connection between Locke on television and Locke in political thought. The show was deep, but not *that* deep. Like Rousseau, Locke rejected Hobbes's presentation of the state of nature as a hellish place from which human beings desperately need to be delivered. At the same time, he proposed a view of the state of nature significantly at odds with Rousseau's presentation.

---

[6]Ibid., bk. 4, chap. 8.

Hobbes had man as a super-predator with highly human desires but subhuman ethics. Rousseau saw him as perhaps the best of the animals with animal-type needs and desires and satisfied with what his habitat offered him. Locke saw the human being in nature as a human, not as an advanced animal, with an awareness of God and his natural law. What made human beings special was their exercise of reason within the context of this natural law.[7]

Because this is an introductory text, we cannot go further without stopping to discuss the idea of the natural law. What is it? With an appropriate tip of the hat to a thinker such as J. Budziszewski, it is the moral law built into the structure of human life that we cannot fail to know.[8] It is a pre-wired, built-in feature of human beings. When I first bring up the natural law with students, they often think I am talking about evolution, the law of gravity, or perhaps something else such as the law of the jungle in which the big eat the small or the fast eat the slow. But those things are not what we mean when we talk about the natural law.

Let's imagine that, five hundred years ago, I had the occasion to meet a man from the other side of the world, a part that was untouched by my own culture. It is highly likely that we would have agreed on certain things. We would have agreed that it is better in general to speak the truth than to lie. We would have affirmed that one should not take innocent life. We would have shared the belief that one should not steal the rightful possessions of others. There are other fundamental matters upon which the two men from opposite sides of the earth with no cultural interaction could have agreed. In *Mere Christianity*, C. S. Lewis noted that it would be hard to imagine a culture in which people would esteem a coward and lose respect for a brave man. At the conclusion of *The Abolition of Man*, he compiled a listing of moral values consistent across religions and cultures. He called this the Tao

[7]John Locke, *Second Treatise of Government*, chap. 2.
[8]J. Budziszewski, *What We Can't Not Know: A Guide* (San Francisco: Ignatius Press, 2011).

(the way).[9] The importance of the existence of natural law goes beyond politics into religion. If there is a *law*, then it would appear to follow that there is a *lawgiver*.

Skeptics about the natural law tend to point to moral practices by other cultures clearly opposite to our own. They highlight these outrages so as to underscore their own belief that culture is purely relative and that laws are a reflection of cultural circumstances more than they are pictures of some morality basic to us all. I think this objection is incorrect. To the extent that I and my foreign counterpart were to disagree upon some fundamental matter, it is likely that our disagreement would not actually have been about the axioms, but with regard to their application. For example, he might have come from a tribal culture that engaged in the sacrifice of virgins to some totemic deity. If I questioned him critically and expressed my dismay that his group sacrificed virgins, he would not likely have said I was wrong and that it is good to kill innocent girls. Instead, he would have replied that his tribe had to do it to satisfy their god. In so doing, he would have offered a justification for their actions. To offer a justification means that one recognizes the wrong and is attempting to give a reason why the choice to engage in the wrong is right under the specific circumstances. As long as someone is justifying an action, he is conceding the moral point with regard to the larger principle.

John Locke was a believer in the natural law. He looked at man, even natural man, and saw a creature distinguished from other creatures in an important way. (Aristotle shared this perception). Man's uniqueness derives from his ability to communicate, discuss, and contemplate matters of right and wrong. We are moral and rational. For Locke, our reason is tied directly to our morality. In fact, to live in accord with morality is to live according to reason. So, men are free in nature, but not absolutely so. In his *Second Treatise of Government* Locke wrote, "The state

---

[9]C. S. Lewis, *The Abolition of Man* (New York: Touchstone, 1996).

of nature has a law of nature to govern it." The substance of this law is greater than Hobbes's "natural right" in which the natural man can do anything he wants or Rousseau's formula of self-preservation and human pity that doesn't stick its neck out too far. Its foundational principle is that "no one ought to harm another in his life, health, liberty, or possessions." Men were made by God and belong to him. We exist for his pleasure and not for anyone else's, not even our own. We may not destroy ourselves or others at our own discretion. This law is one designed for the "peace and preservation of all mankind."[10]

Hobbes imagined a state of nature in which all were in a state of war against all. Locke's state of nature was not equally fearsome. Men live in the state of nature under the natural law, knowing what is right and wrong and conducting themselves accordingly. But this is not a state of nature without sin. Although everyone knows the natural law through the exercise of their ability to reason, some choose to live irrationally and to live the way the animals do. In other words, these violators embrace the ethics of predators. When they make that choice, they divorce themselves from the community of reason and place themselves in a state of war with their fellow men. Where Hobbes saw the state of nature as a state of war, Locke saw the state of nature as something that could be interrupted by a state of war.

When the state of war intrudes thanks to a violation of reason, then justice must be vindicated. But in a state of living prior to civil society, who will set things right? The individual who was wronged in his enjoyment of life and property must do it. In the state of nature, each person holds the *executive power* sufficient to authorize the use of force to kill or capture the wrongdoer. Pragmatic thinkers will see the most obvious problem right away. What if the violator is 6'5" and 275 pounds, while the offended party is 5'7" and 120 pounds soaking wet? The weaker party may

---

[10]Locke, *Second Treatise on Government*, chap. 2.

have the right to use executive power but no practical means for actually vindicating justice. There is a second problem, which is— as Aristotle noted—that we tend to be bad judges in our own cases and thus may not think ourselves at fault when we really are or may believe we have been offended when it is not necessarily so. These problems make the enjoyment of life, liberty, and property less secure than we might like. It is for this reason that we would make a social contract to form a political society.

Political society, according to Locke, must be designed to more properly vindicate justice by protecting our rights. That means any system must address the problems we have identified. The problem of the highly capable offender and/or the weak offended party is resolved by the creation of a government with a law enforcement function. Having something like a police force nullifies advantages lawbreakers might have over their victims and radically increases the likelihood that they will be punished. In addition, political society must have a legislative function to create laws that will be promulgated (publicly posted in obvious places) so that all will be able to know what the laws are and what the penalties are for violating them. Individual cases will be judged by known and indifferent judges. *Indifference* means that judges will not be personally interested in the outcome of the case. This does not mean judges do not care about justice but rather that they will not stand to benefit financially or otherwise by ruling in a particular way.[11]

This government is quite different from the ones proposed by Hobbes, for example, because the state of nature from which men are being saved is so different. Locke's nature is inconvenient and somewhat irregular, not savage and terrifying as it is for Hobbes. Thus, the move from nature to political society does not proceed from the same bargaining premise. If you take Hobbes's deal, then you are trading everything in order to secure the protection of your life. If you take Locke's deal, then you are trading a highly

---

[11]Ibid., chap. 9.

tolerable (but sometimes insecure) life in the state of nature for a better protected and somewhat more regulated existence.

As you can see, the person making the trade on Locke's terms is in a much better position. And Locke's philosophy reflects that difference in the balance of power. Whereas Hobbes's people consent once and forever in a nonrevocable covenant for the protection of their lives, Locke's people consent in an ongoing manner for the protection of their enjoyment of life, liberty, and property. At any time, they may withdraw that consent and return to the pre-political state of being (i.e., the state of nature). The government has only enough power to make men better off in their enjoyment of their rights. That is the only part of freedom people have conceded. People have not traded in those things in which government cannot make them better off.[12]

Freedom of religion is a key example. Both Hobbes and Rousseau would regulate religion (including religious belief). Locke does not propose a government capable of doing so, because it is not part of the subject matter of the contract. In the state of nature, men have the freedom to seek the truth of God and to worship him according to their consciences. For the political society to be as good, men must continue to have that freedom.

The primary thing that is being given up by men is their ability to carry out punishments on their own initiative against those who do wrong. Other than concession of the executive power and the obligation to obey enactments of government highly relevant to protecting the enjoyment of basic rights, men continue to be very nearly as free as they were in nature.[13] Their rights come from God, not the government. When the government fails to protect those rights or violates them, then men are justified in appealing to heaven for victory as they withdraw their consent and launch a revolution.[14]

---

[12]Ibid.
[13]Ibid., chap. 7.
[14]Ibid., chaps. 14 and 19.

What objections might be raised to Locke's proposal? One that was typical in his time was the charge that his doctrine of ever-revocable consent laid the basis for anarchy and constant revolution. He answered in a highly pragmatic fashion. Political revolution is a very big deal. It results in the destruction of property and the loss of human lives. Citizens will not be quick to launch a violent overthrow of the government that is supposed to maintain order. But if they are willing to do so, Locke argues, then it would seem the government has failed in its part of the contract.[15] It is either failing to protect the people in their enjoyment of their rights or it has wrongly usurped some of the people's freedoms. Another objection is to point to the fact that people are often not good judges in their own cases and to suggest that a king is needed to create a proper order. Locke's response was that kings, too, are human beings and are bad judges in their own cases. He included the strikingly Christian question of why would we ever want to greatly empower one of these highly fallible creatures to the exclusion of the rest. It would be far better to remain in the state of nature "wherein men are not bound to submit to the unjust will of another."[16]

Out of this triumvirate, Locke prevails because his reasoning from the state of nature relies upon the most true picture of man. Man is not a happy animal in the wilderness, the way Rousseau would have him, nor is he an intelligent and relentless predator (like something out of *Jurassic Park*) the way Hobbes imagines him. Locke views man in the same way Christian anthropology would have him. He is *sui generis* (unique) among all living creatures. He alone has a conscious perception of God and of the moral law God has built into the world. Locke's man is a man who possesses reason. When he uses his reason, he lives under the terms of the natural law. It is possible for him to disobey. He is fallible,

---

[15]Ibid., chap. 19.
[16]Ibid., chap. 2.

even in the pursuit of justice, because of his self-centeredness. Yet, he recognizes the weaknesses he and others have and is able to conceive of a way to mitigate them. And he is free. He is free and not eager for a king. It is on this foundation that Locke's political society is built. It looks quite a bit like the United States of America. There is some irony there, because when he wrote about the state of nature, Locke observed that all the world was once like America. He meant wild, untamed, and undeveloped.

Locke ends up with a smaller, more restrained government than either Hobbes or Rousseau. His dominant theme is liberty.

BEYOND THE ISLAND OR THE JUNGLE TO BEHIND THE VEIL

John Rawls is probably the most celebrated political thinker of our time. It could be argued that the reason he commands such respect is that he found a new way to conceive politics from the ground up. Instead of writing about men in a state of nature, Rawls imagined man before he is born.

So, here is the picture. You have not yet been born into the world. You stand behind something Rawls called "the veil of ignorance." In this context ignorance refers to your knowledge of what kind of person you will be. You do not know what kind of parents you will have, whether you will be physically healthy, whether you will be weak or strong, whether you are intelligent, whether you will be male or female, what part of the world you will be born into, etc. All you know is that you are a person who will enter the world as an infant and have a life.[17]

Now, look upon the blue orb before you and tell us what sort of political regime we should have. What sorts of rules would you make? Some of them would be easy. Not knowing your race, you would surely prohibit any kind of legalized racial discrimination.

---

[17] John Rawls, *A Theory of Justice* (Cambridge, MA: Harvard University Press, 1999), 11.

Not knowing your sex, you would probably do the same there. Not knowing what kind of physique you would have, you would almost inevitably make rules against violent assaults and in favor of a measure of bodily protection. But what about some of the harder questions? Would you opt for maximum freedom in which winners prosper and losers barely survive? Would you opt for a highly uniform sort of socialism that may provide protection from inequality but could also prevent innovation and social advance? The decision is more complicated than it seems. You might choose a socialist society in which everyone receives the same carefully measured share, but what if you realized that such a society would produce far less overall wealth, innovation, and standards of living for its people? Might you then prefer to take your chances with a more dynamic and free society?

Through his creation of a device such as the veil of ignorance, Rawls revived interest in political philosophy by reminding us what it is all about. Though we can study politics in a scientific (or at least quasi-scientific way), the discipline is still primarily about moral decision making.

One of the reasons Rawls is celebrated is that he is thought to have gotten around the God problem in conceiving a secular idea of justice. As I consider the veil of ignorance, I can't get away from the fact that it looks to me like the picture of a human being about to be sent into the world by his God. And as he is sent, he is asked to contemplate the Golden Rule and say what he thinks it might mean, not knowing whom he may become.

Like the others, Rawls has a dominant theme too. He gives primacy to justice in the form of fairness. And you can see, the veil of ignorance is designed to achieve exactly that.

CONCLUSION

All of the thinkers mentioned in this chapter are important in their own right. The substance of what they wrote and thought shapes what we do and say about politics today. Part of the reason to address them early in the book is to help you think about political philosophy the right way.

One of our problems is that we tend to arrive at politics with preset opinions. We have grown up in families where our parents are either Republicans or Democrats. If we don't get it from our parents, then we often form opinions on the basis of what our friends have to say. And, let's face it, the menu is very simple. You pick A or B with a set of positions pretty much reliably attached to each. Part of the reason things work that way is that we have a winner-take-all form of government that discourages third parties or any other kind of nuance. But another part is that we can be lazy and don't want to take time to think carefully about our political values and how we put them to work. I still recall, to my dismay, the answer a student offered in a community college class when I asked what politicians should do in order to make politics interesting enough for citizens to pay attention. "Make it funny, like *Saturday Night Live*," he suggested, with the wide agreement of his classmates. Today, nearly a decade later, what I thought was a shocking answer is no longer so surprising. Many young people get their political news through snark and satire-based programs such as *The Daily Show* and *The Colbert Report*. Amazingly, many politicians are willing to go on the telecasts. To the extent that we do have serious political reporting, it is often based more on horse race–style dynamics. Who is winning? Who is losing? Who had a good week? Who had a really bad week? We have come a far distance from the *long* and thoughtful debates between opponents such as Lincoln and Douglas.

The goal of political philosophy is to get beyond the shortcuts and templates offered to us by modern politics and to find a way to stand outside and evaluate things with a fresh perspective. That is why the state of nature or something like the veil of ignorance is so valuable. And I suspect that as you read through what some of these thinkers had to say, you thought about things at a much more basic level instead of worrying about whether they comported with your preconceived political identity or the "team" you may feel you are on. The goal is not to win, so much as to decide what is the correct outcome. Even if we fail ultimately to achieve a grand unified theory of political ethics, by having thought carefully about the different values in play, we will almost surely argue better and more substantively. We will also make decisions that are wiser and more sensitive with regard to the common good and human flourishing.

SECTION 2

MAJOR THEMES

4

ORDER, BUT NOT ORDER ALONE

In the last chapter, I highlighted the contributions of the social contract thinkers working from their perceptions of the state of nature. In so doing, brief glimpses of our primary political values shone through: Hobbes with order, Rousseau with equality, Locke with liberty, and (the much later) Rawls with justice.

Let us begin with Hobbes and with order. Hobbes is surely correct to some degree to put such a large premium on having a governing power capable of providing order and the physical safety that comes with it. There is little dispute about that. Indeed, spending for armies and police has probably been the priority throughout much of history. It is a relatively recent phenomenon to have governments spending the lion's share of their resources on social welfare programs as they tend to do today.

Indeed, Martin Luther affirmed the need for peace and order in political society. In his study of the Sermon on the Mount (in the book *On Secular Authority*), he interpreted the admonitions promoting a form of pacifism as binding commands on individual Christians. Thus, if a Christian were about to be attacked or, in fact, were struck, it would be incumbent upon him to passively accept the blow without retaliating. However, the same does not apply to the office of government. Luther wrote that government is necessary to prevent human predators from turning the world into a desert. This government is authorized to shield the innocent from the wicked and to strike the blows, both preventive and retributive, necessary for *the restraint of evil men*.[1]

Government's provision of order is so important that the Christian citizen should be eager to participate in it. Though Luther counseled the Christian to take no steps to protect himself from violence, he should be prepared to take up government office and to participate in the ministry of peace and order. This participation should apply even to the office of hangman if one is needed. Why should this be so? The answer is that one's neighbor needs peace, safety, and order in the same way that he needs food, water, shelter, and air.

Order, though, is not enough. We can understand why by examining the word that often goes with order, which is *peace*. The reason people welcome order, which restricts freedom, is that they hope to enjoy some measure of peace. But what is peace? Maybe the first thing that comes to mind when we think of peace is the absence of conflict. Is that what peace is?

Imagine two families. In the first family, the father is a tyrant. He rages whenever anything fails to please him. Children have learned not to be too loud when he is around. Mother mutes any disagreement. No one ever seriously challenges him on anything, even if they are morally certain he is wrong in a particular case. The wife and children act this way because they know that brooking this man's will in any fashion will lead to heavy verbal and then physical reprisals. As a result, the household experiences very little conflict.

In the second family, the father is kind and gentle. He fulfills his leadership function but is happy to hear the ideas of other members of the family. His wife is his most trusted confidante. He realizes that she will often have a different and sometimes superior perspective than his own. When she is right, he is quick to revisit

---

[1]Martin Luther, "On Secular Authority," in *Luther and Calvin on Secular Authority*, ed. and trans. Harro Hopfl (Cambridge, UK: Cambridge University Press, 1991), 7–15.

his own decisions in order to adapt to points she has offered. This man also realizes that children are not miniature adults. He tolerates a reasonable level of rowdiness and childish behavior. When he corrects them, he does so in a proportionate way and with a view to their edification rather than in order to merely conform them to his will. He listens to their opinions, too, both because they are his children and he cares and because he recognizes that they should have some right to express their thoughts, as well.

Now, given the examples of these two families, which of the two helps us to understand order with peace? The first example shows us a family that unquestionably has order and something that might be mistaken for peace. What we really see there is order paired with an absence of visible conflict. This is not so much peace as it is a facsimile thereof. The political correlate is a totalitarian or authoritarian society in which the government does not tolerate disagreement and is willing to punish severely in order to prevent disagreement or the formation of an alternate consensus. The second example, by contrast, shows us a family that has both order and peace. The peace is real because the members of the family feel respected and heard. They are treated like human beings who have similar rights to the human being who is leading them. This peace is the peace that comes from justice. Members of the family feel they are treated justly, and it is that which leads to true peace.

One of the thinkers who most helps us understand this difference between peace as an absence of visible conflict and peace as a consequence of justice is Augustine. He made that distinction very effectively. Notably, he was perhaps the first great Christian political philosopher. His understanding of peace flowed from his view of human beings as being equal under God. Augustine's reading of Genesis was that man had originally been made to rule over the beasts, not over his fellow man. Therefore, the fall of man and his sinfulness led to the unnatural condition of men ruling over other men. After the fall rational beings rule over rational beings instead of merely ruling the irrational ones.[2] The desire to rule is a consequence of pride. There is only one ruler who actually deserves his place of authority and that is the Lord. Those who rule by lording their authority over their fellow human beings are guilty of attempting to usurp the rightful authority of God.[3]

The point of all this is to demonstrate that order is not enough. Order is not any kind of moral ultimate. The only reason to desire order is to make something else possible. Order is a means to an end. If what order gives us is not good, then we should not continue to uphold that order. For example, a dictator may give us order, but his order may not be worth preserving as we perceive ourselves to lose more by it than we gain. This takes us in the direction John Locke went with his work. Order is there only to secure something else, and something more than mere protection from violent death. What is that something else? Is it freedom? Is it justice?

---

[2] Augustine, *The City of God*, bk. 19, chap. 15.
[3] Ibid., bk. 19, chap. 12.

5

ON FREEDOM (AND LIBERTY)

Order is not enough. It is entirely possible that an unjust order could leave human beings much worse off than they are in the state of nature. Locke and Rousseau agreed on that point. Locke was quite explicit in saying that the only reason to enter into political society and to accept a legal order beyond the natural law put in place by God would be to better secure the enjoyment of one's life, liberty, and property. Remember, both Locke and Rousseau were eager to assert that nature is not such a bad place (paradise in Rousseau's telling!). The reason they made that point was so that they could better resist the elevation of order to the exclusion of freedom.

The dominant themes mentioned so far are deeply intertwined. It is very difficult to speak of freedom without also speaking of order, justice, equality, and other important political values. Nevertheless, for the sake of clarity I will seek to keep them apart as much as I can as we attempt to unravel the knot. So, for now let us think on the matter of freedom.

I am an American. During my childhood (in the 1970s and 1980s), the United States was engaged in a continuous strategic and tactical battle with the old Soviet Union (and it feels good to refer to it that way) for the political fate of the world. I will get into the Soviet vision later, but for our part as Americans, we understood ourselves to be the protectors of freedom during a century of grand totalitarian experiments headed by an impressive rogue's gallery of dictators. As such, we viewed ourselves as the good guys.

Generally speaking, we get a big lump in our throats when we watch a film such as *Braveheart* in which the hero is tortured beyond endurance but never cries out for mercy. Instead, he gathers himself for one final word and manages to triumphantly shout, "Freedom!" just before he dies. That's who we are. We are the freedom lovers.

But this is exactly the place where we tend to stop thinking and just feel things. That makes this point in the discussion especially critical, because it will help us to become more like political philosophers and less like the kind of people who simply listen to people hurling assertions at each other on a television show and mistake it for a good debate.

So, freedom. Is it enough to say that one is a lover of freedom and that freedom is more important than anything else or should we examine the matter further? The question, perhaps, is, what is freedom for? We have many different accounts of the value of freedom in America.

One person might say freedom is important so that we can pursue truth and happiness in our own way. For example, this same person might mention our freedom of religion in which we are able to attend church and meet with fellow believers without any serious state supervision. There is no official dogma and certainly no one forcing citizens to bend the knee in obeisance to a state religion. We are generally free to pursue God and to worship him as we believe is right.

Another person might say freedom is important because a man deserves to be able to reap the benefit from his own creativity and industry. We live in a political system that allows human beings to engage in a wide variety of commercial activities ranging from farming, heavy industry, professional services, artistic and musical pursuits, to any number of other vocations. We are free to succeed and free to fail. And free to reinvent ourselves and try again.

Both of these types of freedom are the kinds John Locke was talking about in his *Letter Concerning Toleration* and in *The Second Treatise of Government*. He argued against legal coercion in spiritual matters because of the tremendous premium he placed upon the individual's ability to search for truth. If government were allowed to prescribe (with force of coercion) what is right with regard to God and the church, what if the government in question were wrong? Would Christians like to see non-Christian nations rigidly insist upon the state's right to define spiritual truth, or would they prefer that the people have the freedom to hear and respond to the gospel? Locke was also a proponent of the concept of private property and thus of the freedom to acquire and hold it. He believed that one of the chief advantages of political society would be better protection for property. How did the common, undifferentiated stuff of God's creation become property? Locke said it happened through the infusion of labor. Work *validates* the right to property.[1] (Though this is the dominant opinion, it is far from the only one. Some argue that private property is a thoroughly scurrilous and unwarranted invention.)

These are noble views of freedom. But what about other ways of looking at the issue? One idea of freedom that has gained substantial currency in America (and in other parts of the world) is freedom in the formula that has become its own Americanized trinity. We call it "sex, drugs, and rock and roll."

This kind of freedom is not so much freedom for the pursuit of truth, or freedom to create and benefit from economic value, but freedom for self-gratification. Freedom for pleasure. Freedom for hedonism. This kind of freedom is at the core of many of our political discussions today. What kind of value do we place upon freedom in this sense? For example, should sex be subject to many

---

[1] John Locke, *Second Treatise of Government*, chap. 5.

kinds of regulation as it once was in the United States? At one time, it was common to have laws barring sex between unmarried adults. There were laws against adultery. There were laws against certain types of sexual acts. The remnants of this code continue on in the form of laws against sex with minors under a certain age. We deal with similar questions with regard to drug usage. There are an amazing array of chemical substances that can be ingested, smoked, inhaled, and injected which produce a variety of effects many people find desirable. The traditional American response has been to ban these substances and to make heavy use of law enforcement to prevent their sale. But many advocates of freedom argue vociferously that this action from the government is unjustified. The sale of medical marijuana in some states represents a protest from this camp of freedom boosters.

And what about freedom for something like the creation, sale, and consumption of pornography? As with laws regulating sexual practices, there have been laws severely restricting pornography. To hear such a thing must be somewhat shocking today, when purveyors of pornography rent billboards in major metropolitan areas and along federal highways, but it is true. And even if the laws hadn't existed, there was so much social stigma attached to buying pornographic materials that many men couldn't gather up the emotional energy to actually make a purchase (this, of course, was before the Internet eliminated any social barriers to using pornography). Today, pornography is protected as a form of free speech and artistic expression. The consensus against it remains in place with regard to child pornography.

Based on these varying descriptions of freedom, we might say there are such things as good and bad freedoms or better and worse freedoms. To the person who might accuse us of being judgmental, our answer is that we can surely find some freedoms virtually every person will find harmful. Clearly, we reject the freedom to kill without strong justification, the freedom to take something from others without their consent, the freedom to intimidate others through the use of force in order to get what one wants. We could multiply these examples. It is quite possible to find freedoms our fellow citizens would almost unanimously reject and would favor proscribing through the device of law and the police.

LIBERTY AND LICENSE

It may be somewhat helpful to think of freedom as something that exists in two categories: liberty and license (a distinction that was mentioned earlier). Liberty might be seen as the "freedom to" or the "freedom for." It is freedom to worship God, freedom to work and benefit from industry, freedom to love and marry, freedom to choose one's vocation, etc. Liberty can be thought of as the freedom to do things that are positive and life enhancing.

When I was a younger Christian, I was confused by the title of one of Martin Luther's writings, *The Freedom of a Christian*. The reason it confused me was that I saw Christianity as something limiting my freedom rather than expanding it. For instance, the Christian does not indulge in sex before or outside of marriage. That would seem to be a contraction of freedom. But Luther did not mean freedom in a general sense of personal discretion. He meant that the Christian gains the freedom to be good in light of Christ's redemptive work. One is trapped in sin (confined by it), but through Christ gains the freedom or the liberty to progress in sanctification. So, we might think of political liberty as a positive freedom in the same sense that Christian liberty is a positive freedom.

License, on the other hand, is a negative type of freedom. Don't think of the word *license* in the same sense as a license to drive or the license to operate a business, but instead in the older sense (such as we find in the finer points of dictionary definition) in which it was used to denote an excessive use of freedom or an intentional disregard for generally accepted rules. License is that "sex, drugs, and rock and roll" type of freedom. It is the assertion of the self and one's preferences to the exclusion of all other considerations. (Rock and roll is taking a bit of an unfair beating in all this labeling. Please forgive its inclusion as a rhetorical device.) Pornography is license. The use of recreational narcotics is a form of license. In some times and in some cultures (including America not so long ago) playing cards at night was considered a form of license! Not all of these rules have the same standing. Games and recreation were often considered sinful in the past because they reduced the availability and fitness of men for much-needed work. It has only been when rules of that sort began to seem arbitrary in a society with much more leisure time that we have thought differently. And these kinds of nuances should be considered carefully.

So, how do we draw the line? What do we value about freedom? How far does it go? What are the reasonable bounds of personal discretion?

THE EVOLUTION OF POLITICAL LIBERTY

In the wake of the French Revolution that occurred at the conclusion of the eighteenth century and the beginning of the nineteenth, Benjamin Constant examined two different concepts of liberty. Rather than thinking of liberty as good or bad, he wrote on the difference between ancient and modern ideas regarding the ideal. In particular, he was trying to respond to the Revolution and to Rousseau, who was an inspiration to the elites who led it. One of the problems with the Revolution and with Rousseau's ideas, Constant concluded, was that they failed to take account of the difference between ancient and modern liberty. Ancient liberty meant having the right to participate in government. Thus, Rousseau upheld the ideal of the direct democracy in which citizens gather en masse to consider the affairs of the republic. Under such a government, with the people's hands firmly on the rudder of the state, the reach of the state was theoretically great and intrusive. What we would think of as personal liberty was not highly valued. Sovereign authority laid claim to everything. Constant criticized this way of thinking about liberty as historically located. To say something is historically located is to say that the practice was fitting for the times in which it was widely practiced but is not equally applicable today. In the case of ancient liberty, the kind of government ruled directly by many citizens and with little respect for personal freedom of action made sense in smaller societies, which had to be highly cohesive and which frequently faced aggression from neighboring states. Ancient liberty is less practicable in modern states with much larger populations.

Constant wrote that modern liberty is more appropriate to the political communities of the current age. We have become masters of our personal lives but inconsequential parts of the exercise of sovereignty. This transition has occurred, in part, because we are commercial societies rather than warlike groups. It is wrong to think that the collective is everything and that the individual is nothing. Thus, the problem with the French Revolution was that it asked the people to sacrifice their individual liberty in exchange for "a theoretical share of an abstract sovereignty." We delegate the job of governing to representatives just as the rich man delegates the running of his business to an agent. We elect and pay them to take care of governing so that we might be free to pursue the things that interest us. They are there to protect our personal liberty of thought and action by governing in a wise and limited fashion. This is far better than making the mistake of allowing the government to promise us happiness and then to authorize it to do what is necessary to achieve it. "As for making ourselves happy, we will take care of that."[2]

Constant's modern liberty is the type with which we are familiar. It is the type most of this chapter has been concerned with,

<hr>

[2]Benjamin Constant, "The Liberty of the Ancients Compared with That of Moderns," 1816. Constant's essay may be found at http://www.uark.edu/depts/comminfo/cambridge/ancients.html.

and it consumes our political discourse today. Arguably the single greatest theorist of that kind of freedom was John Stuart Mill. His *On Liberty* made the case for the maximum freedom possible for individuals both in terms of thought and expression and in terms of action. Specifically, Mill asked questions regarding the nature and limits of the power society may legitimately exercise over the individual. To what extent is government justified in limiting the freedom, both positive and negative, of the individual?

Mill pointed out (as did many other theorists, including Alexis de Tocqueville, the Christian nobleman) that the older type of political liberty was inadequate because even though excessive infringements on personal thought and action might be revoked by the broad governing group, the majority might actually be happy in its intrusions. Indeed, de Tocqueville noted that majority despotism is arguably the worst kind because it carries a moral certitude that dictatorships or oligarchies might well not have. His arresting name for the phenomenon was "administrative despotism."[3] Because society wants to make everyone in its mold, Mill insisted that we must find the limit to political power.

How do we discover that limit? Mill adverted to reason rather than custom or tradition. His justification was that custom is nothing more than an opinion that has survived for a long time. And opinions are only preferences unless they are backed by compelling reasons. Despite what I believe to be the power of Mill's case, it is here that I must make a brief defense of tradition. Though he won't receive much space in this book, Edmund Burke is a voice who should be considered. He argued that tradition and customs represent something like accumulated wisdom. They have survived because they work well for the community over time. In haste to employ cold, abstract reason, those who regard tradition lightly might miss justifications and reasons behind it

---

[3]Alexis de Tocqueville, *Democracy in America*, vol. 2, pt. 4, chap. 6.

that aren't immediately obvious, especially to one not inclined to respect it.[4]

Nevertheless, Mill did an admirable job of applying reason to the question of liberty in the political state. His rationale for maximizing liberty is extremely potent. In the realm of thought and expression, there should be practically no limit at all. We are all seekers of the truth. Certainly, we would rather have the truth if it is available. Thus, we should give individuals the freedom to pursue it and to write and talk about their quest and their findings. By allowing argument from a variety of perspectives, we stand the best chance of making an informed decision about what is good and true. In addition, this kind of liberty, inclusive of liberty of the press, is the best security against tyranny.[5]

To accept any other standard would be to accept the idea that the government is infallible and does not need to entertain contrary views or arguments. While one might object that speaking in this way could render the government paralyzed in indecision, it is not true. The reality is that we can act more confidently when we have really listened to all points of view. Doesn't Mill ring true here? Would you ever consider making a major purchase after listening only to the people who praise the product and completely ignoring those who say there is something wrong with it? Wouldn't you feel much better about your choice if you took the time to decide who had the better argument?

We have already considered some of what John Locke had to say about religious liberty. Mill spoke to some of the same issues, arguing both that government control of religion is an obstacle to spreading the gospel in many lands and that government penalties for atheists result only in gain for atheists who are willing to lie about their beliefs. He also contended that government protection of religion from dispute can turn a living faith into a dead dogma.

---

[4]This is the persistent theme of Burke's *Reflections on the Revolution in France*.
[5]John Stuart Mill, *On Liberty*, chap. 2.

"Both teachers and learners go to sleep when there is no enemy in the field."[6]

While the people of the world can by no means take freedom of thought and expression for granted, it has taken firm root in the intellectual soil of the Western world. The more difficult task is to determine the extent to which we may regulate actions. Mill set forth a simple rule in this regard. He argued that the only valid reason for interfering with liberty is to prevent harm to others. In other words, as long as an individual's actions are only "self-regarding" (that is to say that they don't harm others), then the government has no business interfering with him.[7]

Now, this sharp boundary line for government coercion does not apply to lesser means of reform. We are all free to attempt to convince someone to change his behavior, but we may not compel him through the device of law unless the specific behavior causes us real harm. Any other standard is despotism, Mill insisted. And despotism may work okay for barbarians, but not for people of reason! The only real freedom is to pursue our own good in our own way without interfering with others. This conception of freedom is strikingly modern and seems, in many ways, to have won the day.

Mill's case for freedom is not a purely cynical one in which a person thumbs his nose at society and proclaims like an angry child, "You're not the boss of me!" He believed that freedom actually had an ennobling effect on people. We become stronger by making moral choices. The mind and the conscience are like muscles, which become more stout with exercise. If we are free, we are required to see, to collect information, to discern between sources, to exercise self-control, and to do many other virtuous things. Making choices can actually be painful, which is why many people would rather simply be told what to do.

---

[6]Ibid.
[7]Ibid., chap. 4.

This way of living may be necessary to the kind of creatures we are. Mill asked the arresting question of whether it would be better if we were automatons. Would we view the world in the same way if it was populated by robots who deterministically tilled the fields, planted the corn, sat in rows at churches, sang songs, and prayed at set hours? The glory of life as we understand it is in volition. For this reason, we emphasize freedom. Notably, this is a bet on freedom, hoping for the good to emerge from it. It is freedom in the faith that God has given us faculties of reason and conscience that should be developed through use. The tribute we pay to this freedom is to restrain others only in light of rights of others, which must be respected. To be bound without good reason only creates contempt and resistance in the person restrained.[8]

The practical working out of Mill's system flows fairly easily from his original premises. If freedom means that self-regarding actions should not be limited, then there can be no laws against drinking, using drugs, various sexual practices, and pornography. This freedom would not extend merely to the kinds of things we think of as vice or license. For example, Mill's thought also means that the government could not make laws restraining competition in business. Honest competition does not count as harm to another. Breaking your competitor's display window at the front of his door, on the other hand, would qualify.[9]

Readers thinking about the last paragraph may already be shifting in their seats with some eagerness to address what would appear to be the obvious weaknesses in Mill's position. Isn't narcotic drug use, for instance, something that has effects extending far beyond the drug user, himself? What if a man using marijuana gets into his car while under the influence of the drug and causes a serious accident? Mill would reply that we should make the conduct causing the injury illegal rather than the drug use itself. In

---

[8]Ibid., chap. 3.
[9]Ibid., chap. 5.

other words, smoking marijuana should not be illegal. Driving a car while under the influence of marijuana should be. (This, of course, is exactly how we have dealt with alcohol and explains why many protest that we give alcohol a pass while treating narcotics much more restrictively. The only easy answer there is that we tried banning alcohol and experienced the kind of rebellion Aquinas warned about when government reaches too far in attempting to eliminate vices. Sometimes, cracking down too hard on the little rebellions can lead to much more serious ones.)

Mill would dispose of other dilemmas in a similar fashion. If you say the drug user ends up abusing his wife, then he will say that it should be illegal to abuse one's wife, not illegal to use drugs. He would likewise deal with problems we might raise with other behaviors that we label as vice. To be more explicit, he would ask you to define the injury to others and then would argue that we must simply prohibit the injury to others rather than the underlying behavior that gives rise to the actions which injure people. The correct acts to criminalize include assault, theft, fraud, endangerment, disorderly conduct. Mill used the phrase "self-regarding" to describe these acts. Today, economists talk about actions that produce negative externalities. In other words, some actions create costs that the actor does not experience or account for himself. This is the territory upon which Mill repeatedly focused. Contain the negative externalities and let freedom be the rule for the rest.

Mill further buttressed his case by pointing to areas of life in which we are capable of doing great harm but would not think of limiting individual freedom. The prime example is having children and raising them. There is no limitation on the ability of individuals to reproduce. Citizens are not required to prove that they are fit to be parents, that they can provide for children, or that they will raise them to be decent members of society. So why would we claim to regulate people's lives in areas such as gambling in which it is possible they will be harming only themselves?

So great, in fact, was Mill's concern for freedom that, while he felt strongly that the state should make it possible for every citizen to get an education, he thought the state should not be permitted to actually educate citizens lest it give in to the temptation to indoctrinate citizens with the opinions it wants them to have. Thus, there would be no government schools. Instead, there would be many schools offering their services. The state's only role would be to provide help with tuition and doctrinally neutral testing for quality assurance purposes.[10] (Some readers only just now have found something in Mill with which to agree!)

OBJECTIONS TO MILL

As I wrote before, Mill's case for freedom, even unsavory examples of it, is quite strong. However, there are challenges that can be made to it. One, discussed elegantly by Robert George in his book *Making Men Moral*, was set forth by Lord Devlin.[11] Devlin argued that a society has something like a right of self-defense to protect its culture. Thus, an abstract claim of freedom crashes up against a desire to protect unique features of a culture, the kind that are often expressed in the forms of tradition and customs. Mill's views could wipe out all kinds of restrictions of persons that are cherished by the people of a particular ethnicity or locality. We sometimes see something like that complaint coming from countries that see globalization as nothing more than the heavy-handed export of American individualism into lands with more communal norms. Indeed, this was one of Marx's critiques of capitalism. He noted that the demands of commerce and constantly opening up new markets steadily washed away unique features of local culture. But Millians could still come back with the question, "Yes, traditions, customs, values, they are all important, but are they right? Are their

---

[10]Ibid.
[11]Robert P. George, *Making Men Moral: Civil Liberties and Public Morality* (New York: Oxford University Press, 1993), 48–60.

claims upon the freedom of persons justified?" We look at some local customs, such as female circumcision or the old Indian practice of widows being expected to throw themselves on their husband's funeral pyres, and reject them with quite a bit of confidence.

Another way to argue with Mill is to challenge his premise concerning the idea of self-regarding behavior. Are behaviors such as narcotic drug use, consumption of pornography, and prostitution (to name a few examples) really self-regarding, only? Do they produce no negative externalities? Do they cost other individuals in the broader society nothing?

Some have suggested that no one is really isolated. Individual choices radiate out among us like a candle's light in a dark room or a pebble's far-reaching ripples on the surface of a pond. A drug user, to take one type of person Mill would see free, robs us of his usefulness. Whatever he might have contributed through his life work is diminished. He also sets a bad example for others. Leaving him free to engage in bad behavior runs the risk of legitimizing his choice. He may even try to convince others to join him. We could point out other reasons in favor of prohibition. What about the pain that drug abusers cause their family members? Even if family members aren't being physically abused, they are left with a father, mother, sister, or son in the grip of a drug and sometimes not in their right mind.

And might we ask whether Mill's prescription for punishing bad conduct that results from vice is too easy and too little effective an answer? A drug addict may not respond rationally to the possibility of legal punishment the same way a rational man would. By permitting vice to flourish, don't we destabilize the broader public culture at least a little bit for everyone else? Don't we increase the chances of assaults, thefts, murders, and other crimes? Isn't it potentially the better course of wisdom to attempt to attack the problem at its root? And yes, one can point to the treatment of alcohol and say why not treat all drugs the same way? But the answer could just as easily come back, "We have let one wayward genie out of the bottle. Will we be better off letting out several more and hoping for superior results?"

In addition, there is a question here to be asked about culture. Are there any nonnegotiables besides this insistence upon freedom? Is freedom self-generative or has it emerged from broader systems of religion and morality that need to be respected in a foundational sense (including, to some degree, through laws on things such as personal conduct, marriage, and sex) lest the entire edifice of rights we enjoy come tumbling down? It is not an easy question to answer.

This is not a bad place to bring back Thomas Hobbes. He viewed the social contract as void when the sovereign no longer could protect one's life. So, if captured by an enemy force and placed in a situation where one could not be saved by the sovereign, the obligation of loyalty would cease.[12] But is that a true portrayal of citizenship? I am an American. My citizenship means more to me than just a contract of things I receive and things I give. It goes deeper than that. It is secondary to my citizenship in the kingdom of Christ, but it really counts for something.

Living in a community, whether it be a city, a state, or a nation, means more than just a systematization of rights and duties. The word *culture* derives from *cult* (a word tied to meanings such as worship, cultivation, and refinement). *Religion* derives from *religare* (to bind together). *King* derives from *kin* (relatives). All of this goes back to the Aristotelian idea of civic excellence as opposed to the highly limited notion of the community as a mere mutual defense alliance. How do we strike the proper balance between freedom, the interwoven nature of our lives together, and the visions we have of certain goods toward which we should be striving? Are we moving toward something, trying to embody some ideal, or are we simply yearning to be free to pursue our individual notions of what is good?

---

[12]Thomas Hobbes, *Leviathan*, pt. 2, chap. 21.

6

JUSTICE

If there is anything that can trump freedom as a political value, it is justice rather than mere order. We have already considered the ways in which order is a limited good that can provide much needed stability but must be filled with true peace and real justice (per Augustine) so as to be greater than simple coercion.

The question begging to be asked, of course, is, what is justice? If we could simply answer that, we would have much less to argue about than we do. Let us consider some of the possibilities.

In *The Republic*, Plato spoke through Socrates to reject the insistence of young Thrasymachus that justice is nothing more than "the interest of the stronger."[1] Plato meant that justice is not whatever suits the rich and the powerful in the way the Chinese dictator Mao Zedong suggested when he quipped, "He who has the gold makes the rules." So, here we have a suggestion of what justice is not.

In terms of what justice is, Plato imagined the founding of a new republic in which philosopher-kings and their guardians would rule over lesser castes. Each group would be schooled in its function and taught an origin story to reinforce its role. Justice in this society would mirror justice in the soul. The soul is composed of three elements: reason, will, and appetite. In order for there to be justice, each element must fulfill its own role and respect the proper level of priority. The reason must rule the appetite. It recruits the will to prevail over the more base motivation of desire. A man who is disordered is one in whom the will aids the appetite

---

[1]Plato, *The Republic*, 338b.

in getting what it wants without regard for the demands of reason. Such a person is a disaster both for himself and for a community. Justice, for Plato, is that the philosophers should rule because of their clearer insight into true reality.[2]

Or what about Aristotle? He defined justice as treating equals equally and treating unequals unequally. Of course, then we must ask, equal with regard to what? Unfortunately, we are bad judges in our own cases and will tend to give answers beneficial to ourselves. Some might say equal in wealth. Others might say equal in terms of their families' standing in the community. Maybe some would say equal simply by virtue of being human. Aristotle answers by giving an example. If we had a case full of silver flutes, how would we most wisely distribute them? Should we hand them out to citizens based on their net worth, their last names, their lack of income? No, we should give them to those who have the relevant merit of being good at making music. We are just when we value the correct merit in the right situation.[3]

Ayn Rand, though much maligned by both left and right for her brand of atheistic materialist capitalism, articulated a vision of justice that moves many. Rand saw production as the one great life-affirming activity. Man does not automatically or instinctively derive his sustenance from the earth. He must labor and produce. This was her bedrock and explains why she had such contempt for those who try to gain wealth through either political arrangements or simple pleading. She saw anything other than the production of value as parasitism on every point of the economic spectrum, from the beggar to the bureaucrat to the purveyor of crony capitalism. Though we often associate the American president Herbert Hoover with the phrase "rugged individualism," Rand may have been its purest exponent. Stand on your own two feet or be nothing more than a leech or a second-rater.

---

[2]Ibid., 441–44.
[3]Aristotle, *Politics*, bk. 3, chap. 12.

Occupying a place almost exactly opposite Rand, we could place voices for a more collectivist brand of justice such as Karl Marx, Thorstein Veblen, and John Dewey. Each of the three felt that technological progress and unfair social structures benefit only a few and leave the masses to continue on with lives of hard labor and no real improvement in their quality of life. Each intuited that justice and rationality would (or should) lead to a different kind of society in which changes in government (by revolution or otherwise) would equalize conditions of life among men and women. Their basic case has been substantially undermined by modern conditions in which citizens of developed nations virtually all enjoy levels of nutrition, basic comfort, and access to technology that far exceed the experience of the great majority of persons who have ever lived. However, inheritors of this tradition may point to *relative* deprivation (what the poor lack relative to the better off) instead of *absolute* deprivation to make their case.

We can round out our collection of voices on justice by bringing Augustine back into the picture. One of the things that distinguishes him from the others we have reviewed so far in this chapter is his idea of vertical justice.[4] The justice we have been concerned with to this point could be characterized as horizontal justice. In other words, it is justice in terms of the relationships and arrangements between human persons. Vertical justice is concerned with the acknowledgment of God. In the attempt to make something of these disparate threads, we will examine them in turn, beginning with vertical justice because of the hugely important historic role it has played.

VERTICAL JUSTICE

Vertical justice is based on the idea that we have been created by God and that we, like all of creation, ultimately belong to him.

---

[4]Augustine, *The City of God*, bk. 19, chap. 23.

Therefore, our vision of the good should relate very closely to what God has revealed to us in holy Scriptures and in traditions and reasoning related closely to that revelation.

For most of human history, societies have been organized with something like vertical justice in mind. Keep in mind that vertical justice does not exclude horizontal justice. In fact, vertical obligations typically dictate just treatment of one's fellow human beings (e.g., the brotherhood of men as a consequence of the fatherhood of God). The case for Christianity, for example, as a necessary element in the evolution of the Western world's admirable development of human rights, democracy, and governments of laws is quite strong.

However, in terms of law and politics, vertical justice can be at odds with human freedom in some fairly profound ways. As an example, we might roll out some of the examples of religio-juridical repression carried out by the Catholic Church during parts of the last millennium. We could just as easily point to the severe persecution of Christians by the Roman Empire, which was offended by the Christian refusal to engage in emperor worship. The record of Muslim persecution of nonbelievers continues to be written in the Middle East and Africa.

It is an empirical fact that in a political community of any significant size, there will be individuals and/or sizable minorities who do not fit within the dominant religious group. It is also a fact that history tells a regrettable story about the treatment of those individuals. They have frequently been marginalized, persecuted, and sometimes killed. The history of the Jewish people, who have often wandered and had to fit into other nations, is highly instructive in this regard.

Many theorists review these events and conclude that notions of vertical justice must be ruled out entirely and that political systems must be secular in orientation in order to give reasonable respect to the fact of pluralism (the phenomenon of different beliefs, ethnicities, etc.). I think such a claim goes too far.

The first problem with ruling out vertical justice entirely is that it assumes that religion is religion is religion. In other words, all religions can be counted upon to act in the same repressive ways all the time. That much is obviously untrue. It *may* be the case that Islam, for example, is genetically opposed to permitting non-Islamic citizens to live freely and *equally* within nations it rules. But the same can clearly not be said about Christianity.

One of the distinguishing features of the Christian faith is how it managed to reform itself. When the Christian church first appeared, it had to survive in the vast religious marketplace of the old Roman Empire. The Romans permitted significant diversity as long as each religious group was willing to participate in the cult of emperor worship in addition to worshiping its own deities. Christians would not worship anyone other than God. As a result, they were vigorously persecuted and yet somehow survived to become the religion of the emperor Constantine. Contrary to popular perception, Constantine did not initiate a system of persecution for Roman pagans. He primarily acted to remove the many penalties laid upon Christians and then offered the church favorable treatment in terms of financial subsidies. However, it must be admitted that governments tightly aligned with the Christian church did eventually come around to enforcing conformity with the faith. This policy was looked upon as the loving constraint of heresy. Eventually, the policy would take the form of Inquisitorial investigations and punishments. Some people were banished for heresy. Some were actually burned.

In the sixteenth century, the Reformation broke out in Europe. Men such as Luther, Zwingli, Calvin, and many others challenged the doctrines of the Catholic Church. After much disputation and real war, the Christian faith ended up fractured with different types of Christianity dominant in different nations. France and Spain remained Catholic, for example, while Germany and England became protestant. Initially, the protestants simply followed the traditional program of one king, one people, and one religion. As members of the different varieties of Christian faith migrated to America in the following centuries and churches began to take root, the simple facts of separation from the mother country by an ocean, frontier living, and practical pluralism resulted in the development of the separation of church and state.[5]

Some are now thinking, "Right. And that's the end of vertical justice. Good riddance to it." Not necessarily so. Thomas Kidd has pointed out that the Great Awakening (a period of massive revival in the American colonies) helped lead to church-state separation but clearly could not be said to represent a rejection of the saliency of the faith for all of life.[6] Forces for church-state separation were often motivated by a desire to protect the influence of the church and to keep it pure rather than by a belief that the faith should be privatized or uninterested in political matters.

It is possible to have an institutional separation of church and state such that their financial affairs are separate and there are no official ties between entities while a political community continues to have a strong faith identity. It is not difficult to argue that while the last state disestablishment of the church occurred in the early nineteenth century, America continued to be a Christian nation. As we have extended our pluralism from varieties of Christian belief to many other faiths, that identity has become less prominent, but we are still a nation very much moved by appeals to the Bible, the example of Christ, and Christian tradition. Indeed, it is notable that Martin Luther King Jr.'s "Letter from Birmingham Jail" eloquently appealed to horizontal justice explicitly enabled by God's vertical justice (we should treat each other humanely

---

[5]For a survey of these events and a discussion of their meaning, see Hunter Baker, *The End of Secularism* (Wheaton, IL: Crossway, 2009).
[6]Thomas S. Kidd, *The Great Awakening: The Roots of Evangelical Christianity in Colonial America* (New Haven, CT: Yale University Press, 2007).

because it is God's will that we should do so). His admonition, which should still be ringing in the ears of every Christian man and woman, was that the church must be a *thermostat* (a force to affect the state of things) rather than a *thermometer* (merely a reflection of the state of things).[7] One might argue that to the extent the church acts in the way King suggested, we maintain the tradition of vertical justice.

Most of our battles over the separation of church and state today revolve around the question of just how quasi-official America's dedication to the God of the Bible can be. In general, Americans seem to prefer to maintain an ambivalent stance on the question rather than force some ultimate legal resolution. The cultural and political vibrancy of the church in America relative to its counterparts in Europe is, to some degree, a reflection of the belief of Americans in vertical justice. Certainly, it can be said, though, that the kind of vertical justice enabled by a faith legally reinforced by the government has largely passed into the history of the West. But, it must be noted, the accomplishment of that feat was due in significant part to the efforts of Christians and others working from broadly Christian sensibilities. Indeed, the Baptist church counts its stand for religious liberty as one of its proudest historical achievements.

HORIZONTAL JUSTICE

Horizontal justice is justice between human beings. One of our great arguments is the degree to which horizontal justice must be or should be tied to notions of vertical justice. It could be argued that believing in justice without believing in God is a questionable stance. Indeed, there have been some thinkers who would argue that nothing is real that cannot be scientifically demonstrated and

---

[7]Martin Luther King Jr.'s "Letter from Birmingham Jail" is one of the most famous open letters of all time. It rewards multiple readings and can be found at the website of Stanford's King Center: http://mlk-kpp01.stanford.edu/index.php/encyclopedia/documentsentry/annotated_letter_from_birmingham/.

would view the person demanding justice as little more than a sentimental fool. That camp might say, "Show me justice! Can you measure it? Can you prove it exists? Or is it just one of many social constructs that you believe to be part of reality because it suits you to do so?" Nevertheless, that kind of highly materialistic and *scientistic* (the idea that modern empirical science is the only way to know something) thinking does not correspond to our experience.

A number of commentators have noted that the desire for justice is basic to human beings. If you were to doubt that it is really true that human beings naturally insist on justice, then think about how even very small children protest when they perceive an unfairness. Or imagine how a classroom of diligent students would react if the professor graded their papers in an arbitrary fashion such as by assigning grades by lot rather than on the basis of performance. We all demonstrate our belief in justice if only through our personal outrage when we feel we have been wronged. No one suffers injustice the same way one might accept being caught in a rainstorm.

HORIZONTAL JUSTICE BASED ON CIVIL RIGHTS

When it comes to questions of horizontal justice, there are two primary camps that openly contend with each other. The first group are the partisans of what we might call horizontal justice based on equal civil rights. This is justice designed to remove irrational barriers from the path of persons as they pursue their goals. Thus, the individual should not have to face arbitrary standards as he seeks to gain entrance into educational institutions, interacts with government, courts a mate, applies for employment, or attempts to start a business or join a profession. There should be only one standard in each situation, and that is possessing the merit relevant to the task. If he wants to get into a school, is he smart enough to join the student body and keep up with the assignments? If he wants to marry a woman, is he able to win her heart? If he wants to succeed as a lawyer, does he have the expertise and the talent? These are the only things that matter.

Some readers might be confused by the language here. I have referred to a justice based on civil rights. The modern civil rights movement has come to be identified with a desire for an ever-growing government offering an expanding list of guarantees to groups (often in the form of entitlements to funds or services). When I write about civil rights, I am writing in the spirit in which Martin Luther King Jr. spoke when he expressed his desire that individuals be judged by the content of their character rather than by the color of their skin. The key phrase is "content of their character." King was calling for judgments and rules for people based on merit rather than on arbitrary and irrational categories such as race or ethnicity.

Generally speaking, those who seek horizontal justice based on equality of civil rights do not want the government to spell out a heroic vision of justice to which we should all be recruited unless it is an individualistic vision. They do not typically believe in the value of large government programs designed to foster greater equality of life between persons, because such programs are not based on merit. For them, government is designed to protect individuals from irrational rules and actions that interfere with the operation of meritocracy. To the extent that they think government should seek to deal with more than an equality of rule enforcement, it is to create equality of opportunity. For example, such people might recognize that some children grow up in poor families unfamiliar with habits of success and will never get a college education unless government enacts programs to encourage them to do so through scholarships, loans, and other assistance.

HORIZONTAL JUSTICE BASED ON EQUALITY OF CONDITIONS (THE COLLECTIVIST APPROACH)

The group of horizontal justice seekers concerned with formal civil rights and merit is consistently at odds with a collection of persons who find individualistic norms of justice to be wholly inadequate. In the introductory part of this chapter, I identified Karl Marx, Thorstein Veblen, and John Dewey, but we could easily broaden the list. More collectivist seekers of horizontal justice are both prominent and well represented in America today. In fact, the more collectivist version is probably dominant among the intelligentsia of most developed nations. Martin Luther King Jr. is an example of a person whom this group and the former group both claim. Partisans of equal civil rights note his appeal to achievement limited only by the content of an individual's character. Partisans of equality of conditions agree but insist that had he not died, he would have pushed for a second revolution to bring about goals such as greater income equality.

The narrative here should be relatively familiar. Collectivist horizontal justice seekers take the fact of inequality of resources as an obvious indictment of the status quo. They look at the population of a nation, observe that some individuals have much more money than others, and wonder why the group with less tolerates the state of affairs. Indeed, they suspect, or even outright accuse, the wealthier classes of deliberately exploiting those in the lower classes. As a result, they tend to believe that government should take some action to bring about greater equality of incomes and possessions.

The method by which they mean to redress the differences in wealth is primarily by redistribution. In some cases, redistribution means something as clear and direct as taking funds from one group (such as the labor force through payroll taxes) and giving them to another group, such as a welfare population, in the form of monthly payments. But redistribution takes other forms, as well. The provision of public health insurance is a form of redistribution. So, too, is public housing or a subsidized bus system. Many of these redistributive measures are paid for through payroll taxes that affect everyone working. Some are funded by the progressive income tax. A progressive income tax is one that charges a higher percentage of income as it increases. The progressive income tax pays for aid to the poor and for other programs that benefit all Americans such as national defense, federal law enforcement, and interstate highways. The nature of the progressive tax is such that many Americans, perhaps as many as half of adults, pay no income tax at all (though everyone who works pays the designated payroll taxes for social security, Medicare, and Medicaid). Indeed, some Americans who pay no income taxes actually receive a large direct cash payment, which is a form of a negative income tax. This, too, is redistribution at work.

THE INTERACTION OF THE TWO APPROACHES

Though America, for instance, is not typically thought of as a socialist country, we do, in fact, have a public policy that actively seeks to redistribute wealth. We imagine ourselves as a nation of individualistic justice seekers who want only equal opportunity, but the truth is that the collectivist justice impulse is also fairly strong and has achieved a number of victories. The interplay of these two notions of horizontal justice is constantly in process in our political system. We hear the basic narratives in nearly every battle over domestic political issues and in the run-up to every election. One side wants to pave the way for the individual to achieve his goals without interference. The other wants to make sure no one is left behind on the wagon train to a new frontier.

There are objections to be made to both views. Collective justice seekers say that having a level playing field and nonarbitrary rules would be fine if it could ever be achieved. But they are highly skeptical of ever getting to that place without radically revising the circumstances of masses of people first. As long as some are poor and some are rich, some are from favored minority groups and others are not, some have better upbringings than others, some have better educations, and so on, then we will not have anything like a neutral arena of life that can be governed by simple merit. One doubts, though, whether collective justice seekers could ever be satisfied with a system based on merit even if they were fully convinced of its integrity. They are very much moved by the simple fact of unequal conditions of life, whether or not there are legitimate reasons to explain those conditions in some cases.

In addition, the collective justice seekers would point to the many ways in which we are affected by government policy even when we think of ourselves as independent. A large number of successful persons attended public schools or state universities. Many benefited from federal student loans of special aid set aside for veterans. Homeowners receive the tax benefit of deducting their mortgage interest from their taxes. In addition, we enjoy public roads, parks, libraries, and many other services that we often fail to take into account when we style ourselves as independent actors.

But individual justice seekers have some strong points too. Perhaps the strongest argument they can make comes with regard to redistribution. Exactly why should they give up progressively larger percentages of their earnings so the money can be given to those who have been less successful? The bare fact of the need does not by itself justify a policy of confiscation. And aren't there many important factors that go into being successful? Don't you have to do well in school, delay gratification, make smart decisions, and work hard? Why should someone benefit from another who does all that? What about the old fables such as the little red hen who received no help from others when she did all the work to bake the bread, but then faced many hungry friends when she'd finished? How about the grasshopper who lazed about enjoying life while the ant industriously worked? Should we reward those who make bad decisions with their lives? And isn't there a moral hazard involved in shoring up the results of failure? Don't we encourage people to engage in bad behavior such as drinking to excess, doing drugs, getting pregnant out of wedlock, and developing dependency when we subsidize them with food, housing, health care, and cash payments?

All of these points are probably highly recognizable to you, the readers. They are faithfully repeated with great regularity. One of the worst problems we have is that we fail to acknowledge the resource needs that crop up as we implement our governing vision. On one side, we continue to expand our payments to entitlement programs. On the other, we don't take in enough in taxes to pay for the programs. The result is that with continuous deficit spending we don't deal with reality and keep hard decisions at bay. As things stand now, we have taken the worst thoughts and put them together, as Phillip Johnson argued in *Reason in the Balance* (an underappreciated book about politics from the man who made a reputation first as a Supreme Court clerk and Berkeley law professor and then as a critic of Darwin's theory!). We have combined social welfarism with social *laissez-faire* (which means hands-off). That means that we reserve no right to set moral conditions on the ways people live and simultaneously continue to keep the spigot of government aid turned to the "on" position.[8] The reality is that individual liberty typically requires the exercise of substantial personal virtue to maintain it. And social welfare systems need to require the exercise of virtuous behaviors lest they be overwhelmed (as many are today).

Of late, some have introduced a concept of justice that often receives too little attention. Gideon Strauss of The Center for Public Justice and others recently engaged in a call for "intergenerational justice." Without getting deeply into the substantive details, one of their main points is that irresponsible fiscal policies allow current generations to live better than they really deserve while laying future burdens on those who are young or are yet to

---

[8]Phillip E. Johnson, *Reason in the Balance: The Case Against Naturalism in Science, Law, and Education* (Downers Grove, IL: InterVarsity, 1995), 148.

be born. This, too, is an important matter to consider. Readers of this book should consider the impact of our failure to reconcile our visions of justice with budget realities with justice for future generations. Dying with a lot of debt that must be paid is far from virtuous behavior, yet òur politicians perform the act with regularity.

THE DANGER INHERENT IN CERTAIN VIEWS OF JUSTICE

We usually think of vertical justice as the really dangerous one. The specter of true believers in thrall to visions of vertical justice seeking to impose their views upon us is a frightening one. We imagine terrorists quoting various bits of holy writ as they force knees to bend in submission or cut off heads to make a dramatic point. Certainly, a big part of what the social contract thinkers were trying to do was to establish a basis for politics that would not require religious supervision. The loss of the Catholic monopoly over the church in the wake of the Reformation occasioned tremendous fighting and caused many deaths as communities faced the reality of pluralism in a far more urgent way than they had in the past.

But horizontal justice seeking to equalize the conditions of life have sometimes proven quite frightening too. It is likely that there have never been more ambitious or aggressive attempts to bring about justice based on equality of conditions than the efforts that occurred in the twentieth century. Communist revolutions in Russia, China, Cuba, Cambodia, and elsewhere sought to destroy existing societies that they judged unjust and exploitative and to replace them with new orders based on the brotherhood of man. This brotherhood excluded the older foundation of the fatherhood of God, which was viewed as both unnecessary and an impediment to meaningful social change (as religion was considered a tool used to manipulate and exploit the masses).

The results of those revolutions have been uniformly terrible. Russia's revolution led to the deaths of millions of citizens, broad impoverishment, the extinction of virtually any reasonable intellectual or religious freedom, and the continuation by propaganda and coercion of a poorly functioning society that failed to contribute to human flourishing. China's revolution was likewise brutal in human terms and enabled a madman to place the destinies of millions in thrall to his irrational plans for socialistic progress. China has only recovered to the extent that it has embraced meaningful notions of private property and technocratic variants of capitalism. Cambodia's revolution, though much smaller in scope, was incredibly vicious and proud in its overweening ambition to begin history anew with the year zero. Cuba continues to look as if it were hit with a time-freeze ray that arrested progress around 1959. Citizens do not have meaningful political or civil rights and are said to have "economic rights," which are actually rights to economic subsistence.

These efforts at justice had such horrendous effects in part because of the moral certainty leaders possessed that they were doing the right thing. Is it wrong to want to make sure that all people enjoy equal shares of wealth or much more equal shares? The answer is, not necessarily. The problem is the exercise of human power required to attempt to bring about that situation.

Thomas Sowell treated the problem masterfully in his book *The Quest for Cosmic Justice.* He argued that human equality before the laws, which we have called horizontal justice based on equal civil rights, does not require mass distortion of the organic society. On the other hand, grand visions of equality of conditions *do* require major revisions in causes and effects. Men no longer earn money on the basis of the value they generate. Instead, they are paid in line with the valuations of the political regime that are designed to create equality of wealth. The problem, here, is that a government with the power to so radically reorder our affairs is also a government that has been handed (or that has taken) a gigantic amount of power.[9] And power, much to our regret, can be used for ill as well as for good. Indeed, the record of human affairs suggests that Lord Acton was correct in his association of power with corruption. We might add that great power, in human hands, leads to much misery. The most powerful governments in history have often been the most murderous and the most oppressive.

The basic Christian anthropology of man suggests that man is sinful and probably more likely to do ill when given a great deal of power than to do good. It is with sadness that I report what you, the reader, already know, which is that this anthropology is most likely correct. It stands very nearly at the point of simple empirical truth. If this dynamic were not true, then it would be simple to solve all of our problems. We would need only to find a wise enough and good enough person and give him or her the maximum earthly political power that could be mustered. Sadly, no human institution, not even the church, has proven immune to the soul sickness of the people within. (I note, however, with Richard John Neuhaus that the worst implementers of visions of Christian vertical justice never persecuted with a fraction of the efficiency and ambition exhibited by the murderousness of their secular, collectivist counterparts attempting to bring their own version of the eschaton to pass.)

I hasten to add that briefly working through a roll call of modern totalitarianism designed to achieve horizontal, collectivist justice does not discredit that brand of justice, altogether. Rather, the history of the twentieth century serves as a highly relevant warning. There have been nations that have been much more modest in their efforts to redistribute wealth. Indeed, the United States has embraced something like democratic socialism without really owning up to the fact that we do it. But do note that our own efforts take place within the context of a limited government with

---

[9]Thomas Sowell, *The Quest for Cosmic Justice* (New York: Simon & Schuster, 2001).

definite boundaries on its authority. There are attempts to usher in a new age through the implementation of collectivist justice in which the practitioners do not seek to kill or imprison their opposition, nor do they seek to withdraw the people's ability to support or oppose them as they see fit.

What we do not know, though, is whether redistribution sets forces in motion that will ultimately lead to democratic tyranny. Alexis de Tocqueville, the young French nobleman, observed the movement toward social equality and democracy with a mixture of approval and concern. He felt that God was providentially bringing about the change but feared the effects of human sinfulness. As an example, he noted that majorities sometimes confuse the existence of superior numbers with true morality. Thus, they may confuse their will with what is right. By introducing redistribution into politics, we may teach majorities that it is right to vote themselves benefits from a wealthier minority without due reflection upon the rightness of such a policy. Augustine noted that when a government abandons justice, it may just as well be a band of robbers with badges and costumes conveying authority. For a majority simply to use power to take is not necessarily just. Indeed, the opposite is the easier moral inference. When one observes that in the United States nearly half the adult population is effectively exempt from the income tax, such concerns seem merited.

If we accept the truth about the sinfulness of human beings—and it is the better part of wisdom and experience to do so—then we should perhaps consider revising our expectations of what can be achieved through the institution of government. Instead of setting out our own grand visions of what sort of substantive justice could be created and then imposed upon society like some transparent overlay, perhaps we should simply be more vigilant about injustice, which seems a more certain path. Rather than seeking to confiscate great fortunes and spreading them out to a populace or declaring new measures of the value of work and dictating them to employers in the hopes of creating new and better worlds, it may be far wiser to more vigorously punish forcible assaults and fraudulent schemes. A limited government with very specific mandates can still successfully punish evil. But it takes a Leviathan to envision and enact our dreams. And too often, they become nightmares.

7

A BRIEF ATTEMPT AT DESCRIBING GOOD POLITICS

In the preceding chapters, we considered ideas of order, freedom, and justice, as well as their confluence. Justice and freedom vie for supremacy in our hearts. Our lives together demand some kind of reconciliation of these ideas. Though it will surely not end the ongoing debate, I would like to suggest a proper balance.

As I drove home from the airport after a recent trip, I happened upon a National Public Radio program in which a female journalist related the experience of African women and children attempting to survive amidst a program of genocide in Darfur. What did these women and children need above all else? They needed protection from the immediate threat of harm. They needed to be freed from the burdens of tribal, ethnic, and racial hatreds operating to force them to focus on simply surviving. The brutal reality of what has been happening in Darfur offers greater clarity with regard to the fundamental nature of politics.

Think about Augustine here and the idea of the just peace. True peace exists only with justice. Justice means that human beings don't rule over other human beings as though they were irrational animals. Peace is more full-orbed than the absence of conflict. It encompasses justice. It does not set people against one another. Think also about Luther. The Christian must be willing to suffer all harm that may come to himself without offering resistance. But when offered the opportunity to protect his neighbor in accordance with law, he should come roaring to his defense. Count on Luther to point out that there is little virtue in being meek when faced with someone else's suffering!

True peace, peace with justice, is opposed to the broken order or the false order brought about by the actions and schemes of those who have decided to do evil. Justice thus requires the coercion and restraint of evil men. This is exactly the sort of action that will be required to protect victims such as those in Darfur. Human beings willing to act in the defense of their neighbors, in the defense of peace with justice, must act to restrain the hand of those who would do evil.

Having restrained evil, they must then punish it. The punishment of evil vindicates the interests of those who have suffered and cried out for justice. In addition, the punishment of evil acts serves as notice to others who are considering an attempt to impose their own prideful and ungodly order upon their fellows. In sum, the punishment of evil encourages the wrongdoer to reflect upon the consequences of his actions, causes him to repay the debt he has incurred to victims and to society, and hopefully spurs him to seek forgiveness from both God and man. The word *penitentiary* is a Christian word. The man in jail should be remorseful and hopeful of personal reformation.

And what is the deeper justification for punishment (notice the root of that word *justi*fication)? The deeper justification is the one John Locke identified in his *Second Treatise*. When men choose not to live in accordance with God's natural law of reason, then they forfeit their special status as human beings and identify themselves with the lower orders of nature (the world of animals and predators). At that point, they may be justly coerced, restrained, and even killed. The idea here is that such men have renounced their humanity. They have acted against their God-given status as rational beings.

Christians endorse punishment, among other reasons, out of their respect for the humanity of the wrongdoer. By punishing him, we recognize the dignity of his status as a human being made in the image of God. One would not punish an animal for killing a man. Instead, we would kill the animal to put an end to the threat it poses. Punishment of human beings has a moral purpose for both victim and offender. This approach also accords with a Christian view of punishment, which adds the hope until the last that the offender will repent and ask forgiveness. This act does not necessarily do away with the need for punishment, but it opens the door to redemption.

Another idea follows from this line of reasoning. If some men by their unrighteous acts have made themselves fit subjects for coercion and restraint, then what does that say about those who do not commit wrongs (or at least substantial ones) against others? The logical corollary is that those who do not commit wrongs should be free and uncoerced. They are free because they do what is right. This is the ordered liberty mentioned early on in the book. They have earned the right to be free and uncoerced because they govern themselves. *In other words, if one does justice to others by not harming them through force or fraud, then one should be able to live free of government coercion and expect protection from wrongful coercion by others.*

Why start with those who do wrong and reason back to the freedom deserved by those who do not do wrong? The reason is that we more readily identify justice through its violation and remedy than we do through positive visions. We know when we have suffered an injustice that requires a remedy. We are far less certain about whether positive conditions of justice have been met.

Order, justice, and freedom are clearly related. Justice is the result of the enforcement of a *moral* order that protects the freedom of human beings from malignant interference. We are able to live together in peace and freedom with the government standing by to exercise coercion and restraint upon those who would do wrong.

What about that word *equality*, one we also tend to associate with justice? The most realistic kind of equality we can achieve is an equality before the law. Every citizen should be able to expect the same treatment by the government. Liberty and protection for him who lives rightly. Coercion and punishment for him who does wrong.

Are equality before the law, freedom, and protection from those who would do evil justice enough? The persecuted women and children of Darfur would likely leap at the chance to make a life under such conditions. Another example might be the men and women living in Mexico who currently witness a deadly struggle between the forces of the legitimate government and the drug cartels, which are increasingly armed with sophisticated weapons and are trying to impose their *ungodly* order upon everyone. As these oppressed people hope for justice, they are looking for the government to perform its God-given function in restraining these evil men who willfully commit murder and foment mayhem in local communities. Justice will be done when the government puts down this satanic rebellion against both earthly and heavenly kingdoms.

But there are others, occupying a higher position in whatever is the political analog for Maslow's hierarchy of needs, who would earnestly reject such a conception of justice. Equality before the law is not enough, they might say, because even that results in substantial inequalities in the experience of life. Some have billions of dollars, while others spend most of their lives paying off debts or perhaps worse, are unable to even gain access to credit so as to run up debts. Some will travel the world, while others may never get far from the place of their birth. More prosaically, some will grow up in a home with two parents who love each other and provide a good example, guidance, support, and financial assistance, while others will have an unmarried mother and virtually no ready-made advantages to take into their development of a life and career.

What do those facts tell us about justice? Does the sheer fact of the difference in what some have and others don't justify government intervention to create balance? Once the scales are balanced, say, through substantial redistribution of wealth, how will stratifications be prevented from reemerging? And why do we focus mostly on difference manifested in terms of wealth? Some have better personalities and more rewarding friendships. Others have more natural strength or physical beauty. Some go through life with outstanding health and no allergies. We cannot redistribute these things unless we go the lengths of the absurdity envisioned by Kurt Vonnegut's story "Harrison Bergeron" in which the nation is ruled by the Handicapper General of the United States who finds ways to nullify *every* advantage. It is much easier to redistribute wealth. But does the fact that we *can* redistribute wealth mean that we *should* do it?

The effort to create justice in this more comprehensive sense (if it can, indeed, be called "justice") requires coercion. This coercion is not merely a one-time phenomenon, but instead must be applied in an ongoing effort lest individuals once again settle out in various positions along the social spectrum based on their achievements, habits, skills, natural abilities, work ethic, upbringing, etc. There are serious problems with a view of justice that would require continuous and active coercion (say, through the tax system or the regulatory state). This is especially true if one is inclined to accept the proposition that liberty is the state of equilibrium for virtue and self-government, while coercion is the sanction that must be applied to those who do wrong and disrupt the just peace.

We have arrived (again!) at the central problem of politics in the modern world. There is vast agreement with regard to the need for coercion, restraint, and punishment of the evil that arises from force and fraud. But what about coercion for those who have not done anything to merit having parts of their lives controlled by government? Most of us (at least in the West) live under democracies. Straight majorities or majority coalitions rule. It is a fact that a governing authority with democratic authorization of as small as 50 percent plus a single vote can make laws exerting powerful impact and control on everyone (including the 49.9 percent who did not consent). But *should* they do that? My contention, based on the logic presented so far, is that we have been woefully inattentive to the evil of coercion employed against individuals who have not done wrong.

Majoritarian tyranny (a strong word, but one naturally associated with the easy resort to coercion) was a prime concern of many American founders, which explains the many difficulties purposely built into our constitutional design intended to frustrate easy action. The great chronicler and observer of the young American nation, Alexis de Tocqueville, thought majoritarianism posed a threat potentially greater than that of an absolutist government because of the moral certitude crowds often associate with their numbers. The point is straightforward. Majority decision making is highly logical as a matter of process, but the proper subjects of those decisions is not nearly so obvious. The action of a majority can be just or unjust. The example of modern-day Greece is instructive. Nearly a third of the citizens have government jobs at the time of this writing (2011). Generous retirement packages become available at age sixty. Faced with news of the unsustainability of this state of affairs, citizens riot. If it were possible to solve the problem by confiscating the wealth of citizens making more than a specified sum each year, one supposes a majority of voters would jump at the chance. Would they be right to do so? Of course, no such magic is actually available. Mass confiscations have occurred in other times and places without solving human problems of either scarcity or of inequality in the conditions of living.

No matter how much many Americans, and of late many young evangelicals, would like to think so, large transfers of wealth authorized by a majority of citizens does not create social justice. Rather, it raises serious questions about injustice. Many of those subject to the transfer will have done nothing to merit suffering a financial penalty in order to bring about better conditions for other citizens. They are not suitable subjects of coercion.

Does this argument mean that we should *not* seek to transform the living conditions of all human beings such that no one lacks adequate food, clean water, housing, education, jobs, and other good things? The answer to that question is most emphatically no. The argument for justice in the form of restraint and punishment of wrongdoers and its corollary conclusion that those who do good do not deserve to be coerced simply means that we should not depend on the strong hand of government to achieve the good outcomes identified above for everyone. This form of justice also does not mean that we must of necessity stop with an essentially libertarian form of government, but it does suggest that we should have a strong presumption against legal coercion of those who have done no wrong. We must remember that laws, generally speaking, represent reductions in freedom backed by the state's virtual monopoly on the legal use of force. Force is what lies behind the often friendly face of government action. It should be employed with great reluctance and only when all other solutions have been exhausted.

Here we stand at the core of political philosophy. It is empirically true that voters may impose the will of the majority on a minority of citizens (even a large minority). It is also the case that positive law (the written laws of a nation) may authorize that imposition and that courts would affirm the act. But even with all this official authority, would the imposition be right? When one seeks to answer that question, then one begins to think like a political philosopher.

While I would not go so far as to claim that the model of the political good represented here is perfect or obligatory for one to accept, I do think that any way of looking at politics that fails to take due account of the problem of coercing citizens who do not do wrong is not adequately philosophic.

But what about the hope for a better way of life for all citizens? What about communities working together? How can a low coercion model of the type suggested so far bring about the kind of good life for citizens politicians so often use to regale prospective voters?

The idea of justice as the coercion of wrongdoers, punishment of wrong, and freedom for those who govern themselves leads us back to a simple and valuable distinction set forth by Thomas Paine in *Common Sense* (a highly influential tract of the American Revolution demonstrating regard for the Bible and notably much more friendly to Christian sensibilities than his later *The Age of Reason*). In *Common Sense*, Paine distinguished between society and government.[1]

Society is the voluntary association of human beings. We rationally recognize that something like building a house would take a very long time for a man working alone or might even be beyond his ability. But if he chooses to work with others, he may be able to have a habitable dwelling much faster. He can compensate the others with valuable goods he may possess or by giving his labor and/or knowledge to help with projects they may be interested in pursuing. Because of the much greater ability to live a good life by cooperating with other human beings, we choose to live in society. Society is a positive and voluntary enterprise that results in great blessings for those who participate in it.

Government, on the other hand, is different. Our vices create

---

[1]See chap. 2, n. 3.

the need for government. While it is necessary, we must also fear that it will become a means of suffering.

The key to Paine's model is recognizing that society is the platform upon which we build our positive visions. It is voluntary with participants choosing to join and giving back in a reciprocal way so that they may continue to enjoy the benefits of society with others. Government is merely the remedy for bad behavior in society. It should be a corrector and a marker of boundaries rather than the engine of progress that drives civilization forward through constant application of force or the threat thereof. It is not well suited to serve as the driver of advance, because of the constant temptation to gain success by passing laws or gaining government favor rather than through real achievement. The ability to put together a block of votes is far from synonymous with competence in other critically important areas of social, commercial, and cultural improvement.

Thus, if we want to have a great society, then the way to achieve it may not be to have a program such as "The Great Society," which was set forth by President Lyndon B. Johnson as a series of massive welfare programs in the form of payment to poor, single mothers of children, food stamps, and medical insurance for the poor and elderly. While the intent of the program is admirable, the overall merits of the program have been debatable, at best. Less charitably, we might note that the outcome was a vast increase in the size and powers of the government and substantial damage to the voluntary sector of society. If we keep Paine's distinction between "society" and "government" in mind, the program would better have been called "The Great Government."

Society, by any measure, has taken quite a hit since its enactment in the 1960s. Far fewer children are born to a married mother and father today than was the norm at that time. The divorce rate is much higher. Many more women become pregnant without getting married. There are large segments of the populace in the lower socioeconomic registers in which married fatherhood has nearly disappeared as has the experience of the child seeing the parent get up every day and go to work. Government assistance has become a much more important source of revenue for charitable social service providers and nonprofit entities such as colleges, hospitals, orphanages, rehabilitation programs, and a variety of others.

It is also much less common to see multiple generations living in the same home. This, to some degree, is due to the expectation that seniors can make it on their own with social security and other government assistance. The federal government has gone from being primarily a defender of the nation (50 percent of revenues went to defense in 1960!) to being a provider of social services and entitlements (which are now by far the largest category of expenses in the budget). Critics of "The Great Society" are able to make a compelling case that it diminished cultural and social capital among the poor, established enduring cycles of poverty, and blocked the kind of social mobility that had previously been common for those who were poor. (Myron Magnet's book *The Dream and the Nightmare* is a good place to begin.)

Through the growth of government, we have taken responsibility from the society sector and have transferred it to a giant, collective authority (a more friendly Leviathan). Though the goal is unquestionably benign, the outcome may not be.

Perhaps the best way to illustrate the problem is to highlight one of Aristotle's responses to his teacher, Plato. In *The Republic*, Plato hoped to illustrate the true nature of justice by enlarging the proper relationship of the reason, the will, and the appetite into a model of a whole community. (Some argue he intended the whole thing as a metaphor and not as a plan for a society, but that is not important for our purposes here.) In the community model, there is a class of guardians who are intended to care only for the city rather than for themselves and their particular interests. In order to facilitate that effort, the guardians are to be denied private property. Additionally, they will have no wives and children of their own. All property will be held in common, as will wives and children. The idea is that their only interest will be the general interest. They will care for everyone rather than for their own wives or their own children. On this plan, children might be said to be better off because instead of one set of parents, they will have thousands of attentive adults, all invested in their well-being.[2]

Whether or not the presentation of the guardian class was intended to be metaphorical, Aristotle chose to respond to Plato as though his proposal were a serious one. In his *Politics* he wrote:

> What is common to the greatest number gets the least amount of care. People pay most attention to what is their own: they care less for what is common; or, at any rate, they care for it only to the extent to which each is individually concerned. Even when there is no other cause for inattention, people are more prone to neglect their duty when they think that another is attending to it . . .

Speaking specifically to the question of the family, he noted:

> [Under the plan of *The Republic*] each citizen will have a thousand sons; they will not be the sons of each citizen individually; any son whatever will be equally the son of any father whatever. The result will be that all will neglect all.[3]

In other words, the word *son* loses its meaning when abused in this fashion. The same is true of the concept of property. Utopian (or maybe dystopian) schemes that have attempted to displace traditional notions of family and property have failed even when backed by the full power of a totalitarian state.

The critical insight here is that human beings love the particular rather than the general. When we expand government and

---

[2]Plato, *The Republic*, 447d.
[3]Aristotle, *Politics*, bk. 2, chaps. 3–4.

attempt to accomplish an ever greater proportion of our social goals through its power, we go against the grain of human nature. In other words, we generalize. Family relationships, churches, local charities, and local connections all take on less importance as a purportedly omnicompetent state lays claim to collect and distribute a large (and getting larger) portion of resources. Individuals and local communities lose the joy, blessing, and accountability of right giving and helping as individual virtue generalizes into state provision. Recipients no longer have a tie with the giver, nor do they feel a strong need to respond properly to gifts and help by demonstrating that the aid has had an effect. Proper charity and assistance is degraded into the logic of entitlement. Being entitled is a much more comfortable place to be. It leads to poor stewardship of life and property and creates the conditions for the establishment of enduring cycles of poverty.

If government stays focused on its most critical functions relative to justice and order, then society must act to help bring along those who need help. In doing so, communities will discover that what John Stuart Mill said about localizing government as much as possible applies also to social responsibility for community improvement: to think and act is the equivalent of exercising muscles and helping them grow. Personal and social responsibility, located as near to the source as possible, develop the strength of citizens and of their communities.[4] Moving that responsibility out into some distant Leviathan government results in the atrophy of virtue both among givers and recipients and leads to social atomization.

The Great Government does not produce a great society. A great society has the potential to develop in a political regime that focuses on the basic tasks of government while the voluntary sector flourishes. What is required is that we respect the idea of justice as coercion and restraint for those who do wrong and freedom

---

[4]John Stuart Mill, *On Liberty*, chap. 5.

for those who do no evil, while still remaining committed to making a better life for the people around us.

The first moves are the most immediate. If you are a child, be a respectful child who wants to learn and grow. If you are an adult child, take care of your parents as they age. If you are a husband or a wife, stay committed to your spouse. Work on sustaining a stable and peaceful household in which all the members feel heard, cared for, and respected. If you are a parent, focus on loving your child's other parent, providing financially and emotionally for the child, and encouraging the child in learning. If you are a grandparent, help young parents adjust to the newness of their role and encourage them in the hard work of taking care of children. If you live in a neighborhood, work on getting to know your neighbors and doing favors for each other. If you are a member of a church, focus less on what the church is doing to entertain you and spend time finding out how you can help others both in their quest to know God and by meeting needs in their daily lives. When you engage in business whether as a producer or customer, honor your contracts, pay your bills, and don't take advantage of others. God gives us many offices to occupy in this life. Were we to take all of them seriously, the need (and appetite) for government to fill voids might be far less great.

One part of this equation that perhaps is too little considered is the value of a wholesome example and the damage done by a negative one. Adam Smith wrote about the value of strict religion for poor people in the sense that it often successfully wards off the bad habits that may only inconvenience a rich man but that spell ruin for the family of a poor man. G. K. Chesterton complained about the way the fashionable people modeled their vices for those who have far less ability to cope with the damage done. That problem has only become worse in our own time. One of the problems of the modern church is that we tend to choose a fellowship full of people just like us. How much better would it be for those who are doing well and who have had the power of a good example in their own lives to go to church with those who very much need good role models and encouragement to live godly lives? Instead we flee failure and form cliques of successful people.

If we will take care of the many particulars of living together in society, the larger goods will follow in their wake. The church should be the alternate *civitas* leading the way as a kingdom of voluntary love and commitment.

One of the great questions of political philosophy has been whether government should concern itself primarily with small government in the form of something like a mutual defense alliance, or if it should instead be far more ambitious about achieving some great dream for all people. The question, it turns out, is a false one. Government is armed with the powers of coercion and force because it must be in order to do the job that God has given it, which is to frustrate the designs of those who would do evil. The broader society does not necessarily require those same weapons in order to achieve its goals. Nor is the use of those weapons well justified in many instances. We should be far more keen to work in the voluntary sector than in the coercive one.

ADDITIONAL THOUGHTS ON THE CHRISTIAN CONTRIBUTION

8

FOCUS ON THE CHRISTIAN CONTRIBUTION

This book is part of a series titled Reclaiming the Christian Intellectual Tradition. The series is designed to introduce students and other readers to various academic disciplines as presented by a number of Christian thinkers. In the effort to provide a good foundation in political thought, I have chosen to note Christian influences in the tradition where appropriate rather than to spend the book talking only about the Christian contribution. In a sense, we could say the entire tradition in the West is a marvelous fusion of classical (Greco-Roman) and Christian ideals. The same can be said of the founding influences on the United States of America.

Having briefly, but hopefully meaningfully, covered key political themes such as the family, the state of nature, the social contract, order, justice, freedom, and the political good, it makes sense to speak in a more focused way about the Christian contribution to political thinking. As with everything in a short and introductory text, it will not be comprehensive but will help readers to see how vital the faith has been to the tradition.

One of the things lacking in the classical tradition of political philosophy with its roots in Plato and Aristotle is a sufficient appreciation of *all* human beings. Plato's vision of justice includes virtually freezing some persons in a position on the social hierarchy based on a centralized view of their attributes. For him, some human beings are the soul of the society while others more closely approximate its appetite. Aristotle defended the idea of slavery on the basis that some are simply fitted by nature for that task.

I raise these points not to indict either man or to hold them up for some retroactive censure. There is something ugly about a critic self-righteously doing that from a comfortable spot in the modern world. We owe a debt to Plato and Aristotle, among other things, for their influence on Augustine and Aquinas. Augustine was our first great Christian political thinker.

AUGUSTINE

Students encounter Plato and Aristotle and sometimes wonder how we got from there to where we are now. Specifically, how do you reach a point where human beings take on a much greater inherent value? Augustine, easily one of the great Christian political minds and a star in the constellation of Western thinkers, is a key part of the answer to that question. He holds the distinction of having authored two works that are fixtures in the great literature of the world. This adult convert to Christianity is perhaps best known for his *Confessions*, which continues to be one of the most insightful works of self-disclosure ever written. He is almost as well known for his epic defense of the Christian faith, which he wrote in the face of the imminent decline of the Roman Empire, *The City of God*. What is especially notable, for our purposes, is his emphasis upon the rights and value of all persons. He does not divide the human race into high and low so much as he sees all men beneath the loving and righteous fatherhood of God.

Augustine insisted that the situation in which one man rules over another man as his superior is a consequence of sin, specifically the sin of pride. Before the fall, Augustine wrote in *The City of God*, man was made to be a shepherd rather than a king. He was designed to rule over the animals (irrational creatures) rather than to rule over his fellow men (rational creatures made in God's image). Prior to the awful moment of the first sin, Adam did not even rule over Eve. She was simply his companion. Servitude, both for Eve and for the human race, is a judgment for transgression against God. The servitude is double. Men suffer not only as slaves to other men but also as slaves to sin. In their original condition, neither of these things was true.

Now, after the fall, even the masters are slaves to their own unrighteousness. Nevertheless, God will bring satisfaction. The slave can gain some degree of freedom by resisting sin. He can serve his master with faithful love, knowing that God will bring an end to all unrighteousness and will put all authorities and powers down before his own perfectly just and loving rule. Better to be a slave to a man than to be a slave to sin. There is a message implicit in what Augustine wrote. Those who rule over men with arbitrary force as masters need not examine it for long in order to comprehend it. The unrighteous rule *will be put down*. The fear of God might cause a man to think twice before treating another man as a chattel possession.

The City of God remains one of the most profound reflections on political theory ever offered. One of the outstanding features of Augustine's work is that when he thought about justice, he didn't look at it only from the horizontal perspective of person to person. He was concerned with God's priority as our creator. This goes back to the point made about vertical justice in the chapter on justice. Vertical justice is not just some oppressive situation in which theocrats make unbelievers bow to some ritual nonsense. It could be that, but it is not that for Augustine or for Christians generally. Vertical justice also has to do with righteousness and its pursuit because God himself is righteous and holy.

With his eyes fixed on God as the only truly legitimate authority, Augustine had an unusually clear-eyed and dispassionate view of the state. He was not impressed with the official trappings of the world's governments. To him, even an empire could be nothing more than a giant band of robbers wearing the uniforms of the state. He memorably related a story about a pirate who was captured by Alexander the Great. Alexander asked the pirate who he thought he was, infesting the sea. The pirate responded with equal indignation, asking Alexander who he thought he was, infesting the whole earth!

His sense of God's priority as our creator has some very interesting implications. For example, his indictment of slavery and unjust rule speaks powerfully against the petty totalitarianism of human dictatorships. Pride is what causes the wicked to want to rule. Pride hates equality of fellowship with God. Therefore, the prideful will disrupt the just peace of God and try to impose their own dominion. And sometimes we mistake dominion for peace. The two things are not fungible.

We covered this point earlier in the book through a mental picture of two families (not mine and Ruth's from chapter 1!) demonstrating the difference between the absence of conflict and peace. In the first family, a harsh and unloving father imposes his will on his wife and children through the use of fear and violence. There is no conflict, because the bad father has precluded it. There is no peace either. Peace includes justice. The second family has a father at the head too, but he leads the family with love, temperance, openness, communication, and justice. This second family has real peace.

True peace is the relationship of equals in harmony before God. All have their proper place not because they are higher or lower, but because they have gifts to do particular things. This arrangement is not the same as a network of servile relationships going from top to bottom. Having a gift to supervise doesn't mean one is higher or is a ruler over others.[1]

---

[1] Augustine, *The City of God*, bk. 19, chaps. 12–15.

AQUINAS

Several centuries later, Thomas Aquinas emerged as arguably the single greatest exponent of the concept of natural law. He recognized that awareness of the natural moral law, which he described as being just as true as the fact that the three angles of a triangle add up to 180 degrees, makes human beings special in the whole of creation. In this sense, he elaborated upon the ideas of the man he respected so greatly—Aristotle—as to refer to him simply as "the philosopher."

Aquinas noted that human beings have some share of the eternal reason, and this reason working in them is the natural law. The natural law is "nothing else than an imprint on us of the divine light."[2]

Aquinas observed, as have others, that across cultures, there are some things we all seem to know are right and others we all seem to know are wrong. A man standing in North America and a man in Africa will possess the same basic ideas about morality. Even when there are exceptions, such as Julius Caesar's observation that Germanic tribes seemed to approve of stealing, there is a justification to explain it. The Germanic tribes didn't think it was okay to steal from others in the tribe; only from those outside. And that would be because they saw those outside the tribe as somehow less human than they were.[3] We still have that problem today. Those we dehumanize, like the unborn child, enjoy less extensive rights and protections. Indeed, this was a pathology of the old Greco-Roman world.

Working from this idea of natural law, Aquinas built out a blended jurisprudence. The natural law provides the broad principles or "speculative reason," as he called it. In many cases, this is enough, this law promulgated by God, who has written it on our hearts. But there are a number of more specific cases in which

---

[2]Thomas Aquinas, *Summa Theologiae*, question 91, second article.
[3]Ibid., question 94, fourth article.

the natural law will be too general to provide a solution. Those cases make it clear where human law is needed. These more specific rules, based on our practical reason, must be rooted in the natural law. And the reason to have laws rather than merely judges is to make sure that we set rules while we are removed from a particular situation and we can more effectively rein in our passions.[4] This last idea flowed beautifully from Aristotle to Aquinas as Aristotle noted that men are bad judges in their own case. In other words, rules of decision should be made as much as possible in abstraction from an actual dispute in motion. Imagine a football game in which the rules can be changed in the fourth quarter. Changes in the heat of the moment are too likely to be changes designed to favor some interest. This constitutionalist view of things accords perfectly with the Christian emphasis on the fallen nature of human beings.

Like Augustine, Aquinas insisted that the proper object of law is justice. Without justice, there is no law but, instead, just an arbitrary assertion of some fallible human being. All laws must derive from the just natural law. If not, it is no law at all. Human laws bind the conscience only if they are just.[5] We know they are just if they are truly aimed at the common good and lay burdens on subjects with equality of proportion.

CHRISTIAN DISTINCTIVENESS

This sampling of political thought shows an awareness of the imperfectability of human beings and their sinful nature. Separated from God, we are all capable of becoming self-serving monsters. In the previous chapter, I referenced an NPR interview with a journalist reporting on genocide in Sudan. She reflected Christian sensibilities when she said (and I may paraphrase slightly), "I have come to realize that I am a person of genocide. We are all people of genocide under the right conditions."

---

[4]Ibid.
[5]Ibid., question 95, second article.

Christian political thought sets out a basis for human rights and a hedge against totalitarianism. Augustine's ideas regarding human servitude and God's priority as our creator are especially effective in that sense. So, too, is Aquinas's emphasis on the pre-existence of a natural moral law, which must be at the foundation of political and legal systems. The flowing mixture of Christian and classical sources embraces dispassionate constitutionalism (a regime of preset laws setting out limits to power) as an answer to the sinful nature of human beings and their ability to be overwhelmed by their appetites.

THE CHERRY ON TOP OF WESTERN POLITICAL THOUGHT

The Reverend Dr. Martin Luther King Jr.'s name includes that of the great Reformer Martin Luther, who was a highly significant political thinker in his own right. The original Luther was the great proponent of distinguishing the functions of church and state, thus urging them to persist in their proper roles. Thus, the church must focus on persuasion and care of souls, and the state must justly excel in the protection of life and limb. Dr. King made his own profound contribution to the political thought of the West. He was the single greatest force for racial equality in America through his use of prophetic oration, organization, and creative nonviolence, but also because he wrote the "Letter from Birmingham Jail" (his own version of a great letter posted on a modern Wittenberg door), which sits now like a cherry on top of the great tradition of Western and Christian political thought.

The occasion for the letter was King's imprisonment as a consequence for launching a massive social protest against the rampant segregation of Birmingham, Alabama. He wrote specifically to his fellow clergymen (white clergymen) who questioned his motives in bringing the protest and wondered why he couldn't just wait for conditions to improve. King is impressive in his answer.

The section where he described what it was like to be a black man, woman, or child in the South is heartrending. Part of what he did there was to emphasize the humanity of African-Americans. The more he could establish that, the more likely it was that he could prick the consciences of his readers who were perhaps guilty of dehumanizing or subhumanizing men and women of a different race and thus justifying a lower ethical standard for dealing with them.

His discourse on social and political thought justifying his course of action may have been more powerful still. King began with the matter of choosing to break laws. His fellow clergymen were surprised at his willingness to disobey democratically established statutes. He made the obvious point that blacks, in many cases, had been unable to vote, but he went much deeper in his analysis and defense. First, he considered the nature of law. He acknowledged that he had been an advocate for the obedience of law and that he urged states to follow the Supreme Court's ruling in *Brown v. Board of Education*, which outlawed school segregation. King traced the distinction between breaking some laws and following others to Augustine, who argued that "an unjust law is no law at all." Just laws make a right demand upon the citizen to follow, while unjust statutes create a responsibility to resist.

Dr. King's Christian social and political thought was especially evident in the way he added Scripture and church history into his indictment of those who would counsel him simply to wait. He traced civil disobedience to Shadrach, Meschach, and Abednego's willingly accepting the punishment of death in a fiery furnace as a consequence of choosing God over the earthly sovereign Nebuchadnezzar. King also called attention to the martyrs of the early church who submitted to death at the jaws of hungry lions and on chopping blocks rather than submit to unjust laws that would claim a higher loyalty to that which we owe to our Creator.

The civil rights pioneer built his case out further by looking to Thomas Aquinas. Just laws are those that correspond to the "moral law or the law of God." Segregation is an expression of sinfulness because it denies the image of God imprinted in men and women of all races. It creates a barrier of which the natural law would not take cognizance. Statutes enforcing segregation thus developed an unjust sense of superiority in one race and similarly instilled inferiority in their peers of another race. King also made the important point—easily buttressed by Aquinas's definition of law as being oriented to the common good—that segregation imposes burdens on a minority that the majority chooses not to take upon itself.

Spectacularly bridging the classical and Christian sources, King held up the dual examples of Socrates and Jesus Christ. Both men successfully created incredible tension within the minds of elites in their respective societies. Socrates, the teacher of whom we know only through his student Plato and the man who has sometimes been viewed as a sort of proto-Christian, pushed his commitment to truth so far that he was forced to drink hemlock. Christ offered such a radical challenge to the religious authorities of his day (and indirectly to the empire) that he, too, suffered a death sentence. Both men maintained their innocence but accepted their sentences despite the injustice involved. In setting up this example, King could not have more beautifully and succinctly tied together the two strands of political thought that have formed the tradition in which we live today.

As we know, King's case against institutionalized racism and segregation eventually prevailed in the United States. He left Birmingham Jail and was later assassinated, but his political ideals gained firm purchase in our constitutional regime. Our human laws thus moved into closer alignment with the justice we believe God would have us observe. King's language, as I have demonstrated here, was unapologetically and unflinchingly Christian. In the "Letter from Birmingham Jail," he wrote forcefully as a pastor, modern-day prophet, Christian scholar, and friend of the Western humanist tradition.

King's choice of language is very disappointing to those who embrace him as a progressive political figure but would much prefer he had confined himself to more secular language. In *The End of Secularism*, I recalled the story of a colleague who assured me King would have employed a Marxian critique instead of Christian rhetoric had he at the time possessed adequate sophistication.[6] The reaction is not atypical. I recently had a friendly radio debate with a Christian theologian who urges believers to keep their faith secret and not to bring it into the public square. When I extolled King's "Letter from Birmingham Jail" and its Christian distinctiveness, his response was, "I want to say it's okay when Martin Luther King does it." Secular political philosophers want to come up with a similar rule. The only problem is that it doesn't easily grow out of principle. Far better to allow believers to bring unfettered what they have into the arena of public debate. Persuasion and civility, not some sterile test of secularity, are the correct organic limits on social and political discourse.

---

[6]Hunter Baker, *The End of Secularism* (Wheaton, IL: Crossway, 2009).

9

CONCLUDING THOUGHTS

The most basic question in politics has to do with power. In the ancient world, indeed in the modern world, many political rulers exercised power as though given carte blanche by God or invested with his substance. That can be seen in the Roman emperors, who were worshiped as gods, and also in various Asian emperors of more recent vintage who were supposedly divine. These nations and peoples embraced their own Hobbesian Leviathans in exchange for peace and order. Such a rule was often achieved via conquest.

In the French Revolution, the battle was over who had the power. The revolutionaries forcibly took power from the king and the nobles and gave it, at least in name, to the people. In reality, the power was held by men such as Robespierre and the Committee of Public Safety. Recalling de Tocqueville's insight, we are sufficiently warned that power held in the name of the people is often the most dangerous of all. The use of such power can often be a cynical and oppressive exercise benefiting from the illusion of moral authority.

The French Revolution aimed to take the power away from an elite and give it to the people. Their hope was that if the power of the state could be put in the right hands and wedded to a better philosophical system, then the secret to enduring human happiness might be just around the corner. Around that corner lies Babel. Perhaps worse, around that corner is a field full of mass graves dug and filled by the exponents of enlightened ideologies.

The special genius of the American Revolution and of the American founding was to see that, while it is important to be right about the question of who wields power, another question is at least equally important. And that question is, *how much power is available to the state and the human beings who wield its force?* The American Revolution was a response to a perceived abuse of power, and the American founding revolved around limiting power so that it would be more difficult to abuse.

Christians don't own America or have special privileges in its government. But Christianity has been too important to the nation to ignore. It is sometimes said that England was made by history, while America was made by philosophy. The quip is partially true. America was made by philosophy and theology.

The great political contribution of Christianity has been to place a great value on the irreducible worth and dignity of human beings while also soberly insisting upon their sinful nature. As a result, Christians would see people free but not too powerful. Free to seek God. Restrained by his justice.

QUESTIONS FOR REFLECTION

1) How does politics resemble the family? How is it different? If you had to identify your family with a style of politics, what would it be?

2) When you imagine human beings living in a state of nature, what do you see? How do they treat each other? What kinds of rules do they make? Which one of the major social contract thinkers do you think was most correct? Why?

3) Why is it that order can't stand alone as a political value?

4) Do you agree with the idea of freedom as something that can be positive or negative? What is the relationship between freedom and virtue?

5) What do you make of John Stuart Mill's argument for freedom? Is he right? Is freedom necessary to make life meaningful? Is it necessary to the development of human character? Are the demands of freedom and the demands of culture at odds with one another?

6) Is vertical justice still a relevant concept? If so, how do you see it playing a part in our politics today? Which version of horizontal justice do you think is superior?

7) Is it good for the government to have the power to level out the experience of life for human beings by using its coercive power? Is the use of government power necessary in the quest for a better life for all? What role can the voluntary sector play? Does Thomas Paine's distinction between society and government clarify matters for you? Can you imagine ways to achieve positive change without passing laws?

8) What role do you see Christianity playing in our politics over time? What contribution has it made? Does learning about Martin Luther King Jr.'s "Letter from Birmingham Jail" help you see why taking religion out of politics isn't necessarily a good thing?

9) You have just read a book about political thought. How is it different from reading a book by a talk-radio host or a politician? Try watching some political news programs and commentators. Read some political magazines. Do you see the themes you've read about in this book beginning to emerge? Do you find you can see through the rhetoric to the more foundational issues?

GLOSSARY

absolutist. The character of a government that concentrates power at the top and cannot effectively be challenged.

aristocracy. Rule by a few members of the noble class.

atomization. The loss of social bonds between people such that each person becomes a thoroughly separate unit.

authoritarian. A government with a large degree of control which nevertheless allows many features of cultural life to continue without substantial interference.

chattel. A personal possession (as in chattel slavery).

classical. Referring, in this book, to the height of the Greek and Roman civilizations encapsulating several centuries before and after the birth of Christ.

collectivist. The character of politics that insists on tying the experience of living between people to the authority of a government seeking to create equality of outcomes.

constitutionalism. The idea that political communities must be ruled by preexisting laws rather than by the discretion of rulers.

democracy. Rule by the people through majority vote.

despotism. Arbitrary, powerful rule by the governing authority.

eschaton. The end of history and the realization of perfect justice and happiness.

executive power. The ability of any person to punish offenses committed against him in the state of nature.

heterodox. Out of step with established doctrine.

jurisprudence. Philosophy of laws or a body of laws.

libertarianism. A political philosophy emphasizing individual freedom and minimizing government power.

majoritarian. The character of a government or process by which the majority rules.

meritocracy. The idea that merit (with regard to character and/or skill) should determine success and advancement.

monarchy. Rule by a single royal person.

negative externality. Consequences of actions that affect others uninvolved in the original actions which produced those consequences.

ordered liberty. The relationship between virtue and freedom by which more virtue results in more freedom.

paternal power. The power of a father over a child.

pluralism. The existence and acceptance of many races, ethnicities, religions, opinions, etc., in a community.

positive law. The written law of a political community; law that is a social fact whether or not it accords with some higher law.

Reformation. The sixteenth-century revolution of some parts of the Christian church in Europe against the Catholic Church, which resulted in the emergence of Protestantism.

scientism. The belief that scientific knowledge is completely sufficient and is the only kind of knowledge worth having.

secularism. The philosophy of confining religion to private domains in order to maintain a purportedly neutral community space.

social contract. The exchange of some rights and freedoms possessed by individuals in the state of nature for the superior protection of others by government.

socialist. The character of political insistence on the government's ability to equalize the experience of living among all citizens.

state of nature. Life for human beings in a pre-political situation, as in the wilderness.

state of war. The conflict that may arise in the state of nature between human beings who want the same thing or when one human being commits a wrong against another.

totalitarian. A government with complete control over all facets of life in a community.

triumvirate. A group of three leaders or highly notable figures.

Western civilization. Generally referring to the course of political and social development beginning from the civilization of the Greeks and Romans and continuing through European Christendom, the Reformation and the Renaissance, and the modern period.

INDEX

✚ CHECK OUT THE OTHER BOOKS IN THE
**RECLAIMING THE CHRISTIAN
INTELLECTUAL TRADITION SERIES**

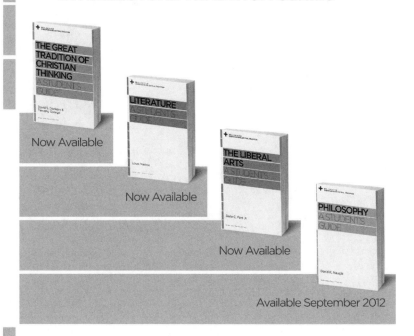

Now Available

Now Available

Now Available

Available September 2012